CMA Publication No. 244

Assessing Policy Interventions in Agri-Business and Allied Sector Credit versus Credit Plus Approach for Livelihood Promotion

CMA Publication No. 244

Assessing Policy Interventions in Agri-Business and Allied Sector Credit versus Credit Plus Approach for Livelihood Promotion

Samar K. Datta
Debdatta Pal
Anirban Ghosh
Souvik Naskar
Tapas Layek

ALLIED PUBLISHERS PVT. LTD.

New Delhi • Mumbai • Kolkata • Lucknow • Chennai
Nagpur • Bangalore • Hyderabad • Ahmedabad

ALLIED PUBLISHERS PRIVATE LIMITED

1/13-14 Asaf Ali Road, **New Delhi**–110002
Ph.: 011-23239001 • E-mail: delhi.books@alliedpublishers.com

47/9 Prag Narain Road, Near Kalyan Bhawan, **Lucknow**–226001
Ph.: 0522-2209942 • E-mail: lko.books@alliedpublishers.com

17 Chittaranjan Avenue, **Kolkata**–700072
Ph.: 033-22129618 • E-mail: cal.books@alliedpublishers.com

15 J.N. Heredia Marg, Ballard Estate, **Mumbai**–400001
Ph.: 022-42126969 • E-mail: mumbai.books@alliedpublishers.com

60 Shiv Sunder Apartments (Ground Floor), Central Bazar Road,
Bajaj Nagar, **Nagpur**–440010
Ph.: 0712-2234210 • E-mail: ngp.books@alliedpublishers.com

F-1 Sun House (First Floor), C.G. Road, Navrangpura,
Ellisbridge P.O., **Ahmedabad**–380006
Ph.: 079-26465916 • E-mail: ahmbd.books@alliedpublishers.com

751 Anna Salai, **Chennai**–600002
Ph.: 044-28523938 • E-mail: chennai.books@alliedpublishers.com

5th Main Road, Gandhinagar, **Bangalore**–560009
Ph.: 080-22262081 • E-mail: bngl.books@alliedpublishers.com

3-2-844/6 & 7 Kachiguda Station Road, **Hyderabad**–500027
Ph.: 040-24619079 • E-mail: hyd.books@alliedpublishers.com

Website: www.alliedpublishers.com

ISBN: 978-81-8424-861-6

Published by Sunil Sachdev and printed by Ravi Sachdev at Allied Publishers Pvt. Ltd. (Printing Division), A-104 Mayapuri Phase II, New Delhi-110064

Foreword

The Centre for Management in Agriculture (CMA) at the Indian Institute of Management, Ahmedabad (IIMA) has since its inception been actively engaged in applied, policy and problem-solving research in agri-business, rural and allied sectors. The research studies on a wide range of problems that are related to fields such as input supply management, commodity systems, procurement, agro-processing, rural credit, agricultural exports, livestock, fisheries, forestry, food safety and quality issues, indigenous innovations, and international trade including WTO issues; have been carried out over the years.

The present study sponsored by the Ministry of Agriculture, Govt. of India has attempted to assess policy interventions in agri-business and allied sector credit versus credit plus approach for livelihood promotion. Through analysis of primary data collected from a carefully selected sample of 350 households from three states of West Bengal, Chhatisgarh and Gujarat, this study has arrived at the following four conclusions: different credit sources are not always in competitive relation with each other; no single source has point wise superiority over others; semi-formal and informal credit sources arise and function steadily without much of government subsidies just because they enjoy certain comparative advantages in local scenarios, and often act in response to certain glaring and persistent shortfalls of formal sector credit; and given rationing of loan by formal sources, these sources often come to the rescue of rural borrowers, thus implying that these sources stand in complementary relationship with each other from the viewpoint of a resource-poor or even any typical rural borrower.

We believe the findings as well as the policy prescriptions would assist evolution of a sound and healthy credit policy in India.

Sukhpal Singh
Chairperson
Centre for Management in Agriculture
Ahmedabad

Preface

The lead author of this manuscript, being impressed with the credit plus activities of several well-known multi-purpose cooperative societies (like Amalsad in South Gujarat, and Mulukanoor and Pathangal in Andhra Pradesh) and an NBSC-MFI named Basix, decided to launch a study from CMA side to highlight the importance of credit plus services and the need for livelihood promotion activities. Although this study was accepted by CMA in August 2008, the Ministry imposed 2–3 rounds of revisions over a fairly large span of time to include the impact of Loan Waiver Scheme of 2008 as well as the role of extension in this context. Though operation of this project got delayed due to this revision, the Ministry was happy that the undersigned was taking up a project similar to another one he had undertaken almost a decade ago along with Prof. M.S. Sriram. However, unlike in the earlier occasion, the response this time from the other Agro-Economic Research Centres, which the Ministry wanted to take up in some of their respective states was lacklustre, resulting in only one Centre taking up this project only in one more state—namely, Maharashtra, again with a gap.

This manuscript brings out the results from a sample of 350 observations of households across the states of West Bengal, Chhattisgarh and Gujarat. The report based on a more comprehensive data set, which includes the states of Maharashtra (undertaken by the Pune Centre), and the states of Andhra Pradesh and Tamil Nadu (undertaken by Prof. Debdatta Pal, the then FPM student at IIM, Ahmedabad for development of his FPM dissertation) is expected to be coming out soon, based on a larger sample site of 600 households and a more rigorous statistical exercise.

Thanks to the interest of Prof. Pal, now a faculty at IIM, Indore to pursue a topic out of the data set of this project in his FPM dissertation, and the interest of the other co-authors, a fairly comprehensive questionnaire could be prepared and canvassed through the hard work of the team members. It also provided immense satisfaction to the undersigned, as at least one of the co-authors made rigorous use of the data so generated to extract lessons for formal sector banks in the management of interlinked transactions. This incident is as noteworthy as a similar one, when Dr. Basab Dasgupta, an ex-Research Assistant currently at World Bank, Washington D.C., made use of the data set of the earlier project almost a decade ago to write his Ph.D. dissertation at University of Connecticut in USA. These two instances bring out several important lessons, which the undersigned would like to highlight at the fag end of his career at IIMA, in the interest of both MoA and CMA.

As the undersigned had once pointed out to the-then, Union Minister of Agriculture, Mr. Buta Singh and the-then Prime Minister of India, Mr. Rajiv Gandhi, the small data sets created by the Agro-Economic Research Centres and Units are too valuable to be ignored for further rigorous analysis and extraction of knowledge for policy making. It was great that both these leaders had accepted the suggestion and wanted to convert the Agro-Economic Centre at Santiniketan into a National Centre to perform this task of dissemination of these data sets as one of its activities. Though this dream failed due to some insurmountable opposition from expected sources, the issue still remains valid and needs to be addressed—mainly by the Directorate of Economics and Statistics within MoA. It may be recalled in this connection that the Centre for Rural Studies at Sussex University in U.K. became famous when it published the village survey data of Agro-Economic Research Centres of MoA under the leadership of Prof. Michael Lipten and Prof. Biplab Das Gupta. Late Dr. S.R. Sen, ex-ESA too had similar ideas, as he spoke to the undersigned on several occasions.

From IIMA side, with the gradual shrinkage of CMA's faculty size, on the one hand, and very occasional availability of an FPM student like Debdatta Pal to make optimal use of the generated data sets, on the other, it is becoming increasingly difficult, if not altogether impossible, to generate valuable field based data for rigorous statistical analysis—not to speak of publications out of them in national and international forum, to carry loud messages from Indian countryside to the rest of the world. Not only with advancement of age, but also with increasing in-house demand for teaching more and more class sessions, these data sets, even if created, tend to remain unutilized or underutilized. The undersigned will feel extremely grateful, if any visionary reader within the relevant quarters takes cognizance of this observation and tries his bit to avoid this loss of national resources.

The undersigned wants to record his gratitude to three reviewers—Prof. Anand Vadivelu of the Institute of Economic Growth, Delhi, Mr. K.G. Karmakar, ex-MD of NABARD and Mr. Chandrasekhar Ghosh, CMD of Bandhan—for carefully going through this manuscript and providing useful suggestions for improvement. Dr. Sankar Datta of BASIX

Livelihood School, Dr. Sanket Thakur of Agricons Agropreneurs, Raipur, Chhattisgarh, Dr. R.K. Singh of SIRD, Chhatisgarh and Mr. Dinanadhu Das of Youth Development Center at Sandeshkhali-II in West Bengal provided inspirations and support throughout. Ms. Priyanjali Sinha and Ms. Ramany Vijayapalan provided necessary secretarial support, while Mr. Avik Chakraborti did careful checking of all modifications and corrections made on the final manuscript. The authors alone are however responsible for all remaining errors of omission and commission committed in this study.

Prof. Samar K. Datta
(on behalf of the authors)
Centre for Management in Agriculture
Indian Institute of Management, Ahmedabad

Contents

List of Tables

CHAPTER 1

Introduction

1.1 BACKGROUND

India continues to be a predominantly agrarian economy with agriculture's contribution of about one fifth to the GDP and about two-thirds in terms of employment of the rural population. Indian agriculture plays a unique role in food security, employment creation and poverty alleviation and in the macroeconomic framework—through maintenance of a fairly low level of commodity prices, providing cheap labor for expanding industrial and services sector and providing both direct and indirect foreign exchange earnings. The Rural Non-Farm Sector (RNFS) has also emerged as one of the key areas for country's economic development with high potential for generating employment and increased income in the rural areas. Therefore, the need for timely and adequate credit as a critical input to agriculture and allied activities as well as to non-farm sector assumes special significance.

Recognizing the importance of the rural economy in India's development, the Government and Reserve Bank of India (RBI) have played a vital role in creating a broad-based institutional framework for catering to the increasing credit requirements of the sector. Rural credit policy of government essentially lays emphasis on augmenting credit flow to rural farm and non-farm borrowers, as well as providing them credit on more favorable terms through credit planning, adoption of region-specific strategies, rationalization of lending policies and procedures, and bringing down the cost of borrowing. Bank credit is available to farmers in the form of short-term credit for financing crop production programs and in the form of medium-term/long-term credit for financing capital investment in agriculture and allied activities like land development including purchase of land, minor irrigation, farm mechanization, dairy development, poultry, animal husbandry, fisheries, plantation, and horticulture. Loans are also made available for storage, processing and marketing of agricultural produce.

The formal sector credit delivery channels include (nationalized) commercial banks with rural credit targets, regional rural banks, a three tier cooperative credit structure for short term loans with a parallel structure for long term loans, and an administered interest rate structure. The credit delivery mechanisms include the subsidized schematic lendings through Prime Minister Rojgar Yojna (PMRY), credit through Differential Rate of Interest (DRI), subsidized loan to particular social groups (i.e., SC/ST), providing revolving fund and subsidy for economic activity through an integrated programme for self-employment of the rural poor by organizing them into Self Help Groups (i.e., Swarna Jayanti Gram Swarozgar Yojna) and also Short Term Credit to farmers through interest subvention schemes.

However, the reality is far from expectation. The All India Debt and Investment Survey as on June 30, 2002 (NSSO, 2005) revealed that dependence on institutional credit sources reduced from 66.3 per cent in 1991 to 57.7 per cent in 2002. The results of World Bank's—Rural Finance Access Survey (2003) found that only 21 per cent of rural households are indebted with formal financial institutions leaving 79 per cent with informal sources (Table 1.1).

Table 1.1: Household Category Wise Access to Credit from Formal Sources

Indicator	*Marginal*	*Small*	*Large*	*Commercial*	*Others*	*Total*
With formal loan outstanding	12.97	30.79	44.36	16.78	29.47	21.01
Without formal loan	87.03	69.21	55.64	83.22	70.53	78.99

Note: Marginal farming households = landholding = < 1 ha.; small = 1 to 2 ha.; large farms = > 2 ha.; commercial households = with or without land but with income from non-farm sources exceeding half of total household income; others = mixed households with land and non-farm commercial incomes but the latter being less than half of their total household income.

Source: World Bank—RFAS (2003).

The large scale exclusion from formal credit delivery mechanism thus points out that there are still numerous systemic weaknesses lying within the widespread formal credit delivery mechanism. The base of the cooperative credit structure (PACS) is in precarious financial health, with large scale defaults by members. While coverage in terms of members is impressive, only a small fraction of members are actually borrowers. Administered rates for the commercial banking structure has led to credit rationing with the sanctioning of loans taking place through political processes rather than on criterion of economic efficiency. Political and bureaucratic interference has also slackened incentives to ensure repayments, with consequent large scale defaults in the commercial banking sector as well, necessitating periodic loan write-offs and debt forgiveness schemes.

Asymmetric information between borrower and lender creates issues of adverse selection, moral hazard and opportunistic behavior on the part of both the borrower and the lender. The typical solution to the incentive problem in the formal credit sector has been for the lender to insist on collateral for the provision of loans. This insistence on collateral meant that poor rural borrowers without marketable collateral had to be excluded from the formal credit delivery mechanism. The rural moneylender has obviated the need for collateral by resorting to strategies such as interlinkage of contracts (at terms unfavorable to borrowers), as well as the threat of withholding further access to credit in cases of default, and using coercive methods to ensure repayment. However, neither situation is optimal—on the one hand, credit rationing in the formal sector, and on the other hand, expropriation and immiserization of borrowers in the informal sector.

While default by borrower may result from unforeseen shocks—output failures, adverse price fluctuations and/or capacity failures, and hence may be non-willful on the part of the borrower, it may also be willful in nature, caused by opportunistic behavior by the borrower. So, smooth functioning of the rural credit market necessarily calls for an efficient operational model that can simultaneously take care of both willful and non-willful defaults of the borrowers.

The preferred approach of the government-backed credit infrastructure in handling the problems of credit has been the partial equilibrium approach, with individual interventions aimed at handling simultaneously one or at most a subset of the myriad problems of rural credit. For example, government credit interventions have more often than not failed to simultaneously address imperfections in the technology, risk, input and output markets, all of which have a bearing on the viability of the credit intervention.

The 'theory of second best' tells us that attempting to address the imperfections in the credit market alone while ignoring other market imperfecttions is usually insufficient to restore optimality[1]. It is therefore no

[1] "In welfare economics, the theory of the second best concerns what happens when one or more optimality conditions cannot be satisfied". Thus, "if one optimality condition in an economic model cannot be satisfied, it is possible that the next

surprise that most of the credit interventions so far have had limited success at best, whether viewed from the point of view of the lender or the borrower. Table 1.2 illustrates the limited efforts of various institutions in handling the sources of risk that confront borrowers.

Table 1.2: Various Efforts at Handling Borrower Risks

Credit Delivery Mechanism	*Risk Covered by Creditor*			
	Non-Willful Default[2]			*Willful Default*
	Production Risk	*Price Risk*	*Capacity Risk*	
Village Moneylenders, providing loans against marketable/non-marketable collateral	Not covered. Incidence of risk passed on to debtor through extra-economic coercion using socio-political influence, and interlinking factor markets.	Not covered. Incidence of risk passed on to debtor through extra-economic coercion using socio-political influence, and interlinking factor markets.	Not covered. Incidence of risk passed on to debtor through extra-economic coercion using socio-political influence, and interlinking factor markets.	Covered, using intimate knowledge about credit-absorption and income generating capacities of borrowers.
Primary Agricultural Credit Co-operative Societies (PACS), demanding only marketable collateral	Not covered, unless risk mitigated for borrower through rescheduling of debts in case of inability to repay.	Covered to an extent if some input supply and output marketing services provided. Political and bureaucratic interference, however, reduce efficiency in handling risk.	Covered to the extent that certain inputs are bundled with accident insurance.	Covered, using intimate knowledge about credit-absorption and income generating capacities of borrowers.

Table contd...

best solution involves changing other variables away from the ones that are usually assumed to be optimal. ... This suggests that economists need to study the details of the situation before jumping to the theory-based conclusion that an improvement in market perfection in one area implies a global improvement in efficiency".

Source: http://en.wikipedia.org/wiki/Theory_of_the_second_best

[2] Non-willful default may also arise from quality and business environment changes beyond the control of the borrower or the lender.

Table 1.2 contd...

Credit Delivery Mechanism	*Risk Covered by Creditor*			
	Non-Willful Default[2]			*Willful Default*
	Production Risk	*Price Risk*	*Capacity Risk*	
State-owned Commercial and Regional Rural Banks, demanding only marketable collateral	Not covered. Risk mitigated to some extent through debt rescheduling and even debt waivers.	Not covered. Risk mitigated to some extent through debt rescheduling and even debt waivers.	Not covered. Risk mitigated to some extent through debt rescheduling and even debt waivers.	Can't check willful default in the absence of intimate knowledge about credit-absorption and income generating capacities of borrowers. Political and bureaucratic interventions further eroded willingness and ability to reduce willful default.
Traditional Micro-finance Institutions, using trust and group cohesion as collective collateral	Not covered. Incidence of risks passed onto debtors with little provision to reduce the severity of risks through debt rescheduling. However, risks are small due to low scale of operation.	Not covered. Incidence of risks passed onto debtors, with little provision to reduce the severity of risks through debt rescheduling. However, risks are small due to low scale of operation.	Not covered. Incidence of risks passed onto the debtors, with little provision to reduce the severity of risks through debt rescheduling. However, risks are small due to low scale of operation.	Use of social collateral as well as group monitoring mechanism led to considerable reduction in possibilities of willful default.

Indeed, the bankruptcy of this partial equilibrium approach is highlighted by the necessity for repeated debt forgiveness schemes on account of periodic widespread inability of farmers to repay loans, as well as increase-ing instances of agrarian distress. The Johl Committee Report on agrarian distress highlighted the failure of credit market interventions to simultaneously address other market imperfections. Johl (2006, p. 47) observed that "Although credit is a very important factor in distress amelioration, provision of mere credit without proper evaluation of the credit needs and repaying capacity of the borrowers will only worsen the indebtedness situation of the farm sector." In this context, the need of the hour is to demonstrate a successful credit intervention that treats the problem of rural credit in a holistic fashion by simultaneously addressing all market imperfections. However, government administrative failure to manage credit market interventions due to high transaction costs, elite capture etc. may reinforce, rather than tackle, credit market failure. The problems of government failure seem to be more serious when simultaneous actions in multiple fronts—both credit and credit-complementary services are—called for.

Against this background, it has become necessary to evaluate the relative strengths and weaknesses of traditional (only) credit market intervention policy—mostly pursued by government agencies—vis-à-vis the emerging 'credit plus' approach, as picked up by some new generation organizations in the non-government sector. The purpose of this study is to bring out the differences between the two approaches (i.e., their efficiency, equity, sustainability properties, besides socio-economic impacts) not only in conceptual terms but also in terms of a rigorous empirical analysis against a suitable data set.

1.2 AN OVERVIEW OF FORMAL SECTOR CREDIT INTERVENTIONS

The evolution of institutional credit to agriculture could be broadly classified into four distinct phases—1904–1969 (predominance of co-operatives and setting up of RBI), 1969–1975 [nationalization of commercial banks and setting up of Regional Rural Banks (RRBs)], 1975–1990 (setting up of NABARD) and from 1991 onwards (financial sector reforms). The genesis of institutional involvement in the sphere of rural credit could be traced back to the enactment of the Cooperative Societies Act in 1904. The establishment of the RBI in 1935 reinforced the process of institutional development for agricultural credit. The RBI is perhaps the first central bank in the world to have taken interest in the matters related to agriculture and agricultural credit, and it continues to do so (Reddy, 2001)[3].

Rural credit policies in India have been reviewed from time to time to maintain pace with the changing requirements of the rural sector. The

[3] Reddy, Y.V. (2001). Indian Agriculture and Reform: Concern, Issues and Agenda. RBI Bulletin, March.

target for individual domestic Scheduled Commercial Bank (SCB) for priority sector lending as well as agricultural lending has been stipulated at 40 per cent and 18 per cent respectively of Adjusted Net Bank Credit (ANBC) or credit equivalent amount of Off-Balance Sheet Exposure, whichever is higher (RBI, 2008)[4].

With the general idea of improving the farmer's timely and adequate accessibility to bank credit, simplifying credit delivery mechanism and providing more flexibility in use of credit by adopting whole farm approach, the concept of Kisan Credit Card (KCC) was first mooted in the Union Budget of 1998–99 and started from that year. The current design of the scheme takes the consideration of the past credit performance of the farmer borrower, his cropping pattern and also some element of his consumption needs in fixing the credit limits. The borrower is required to get this card to zero balance once in a year. Revolving cash credit facility allows any number of withdrawals and repayments within the limit. Although the card was initially oriented towards short-term credit, in the present design, it looks at those sub components—short term production credit, working capital credit and term credit, with the validity of the card extendable to a maximum period of 5 years. Thus, currently, it has provision that a credit can be extended up to 5 year maturity period. The card holders are also covered by insurance.

Since the financial sector reforms from 1991, Government has appointed several expert committees on rural credit for detailed analysis of the credit delivery mechanisms that have come out with several suggestions ranging from ground level revamping measures to policy interventions. In the process, the cooperative credit structure has been thoroughly examined by a number of committees—Capoor Committee (2000), Vyas Committee (2004), Vaidyanathan Committee (2004) and its weaknesses brought out for possible remedial actions. The Capoor Committee (2000) advised re-engineering around four major points—namely, member driven co-operatives, strengthening of resource base, especially capital, structural changes and improved management. The Vyas Committee (2002), on the other hand, recommended (a) government financial support; (b) replacing State Cooperative Acts by Model Act to achieve effective cooperative governance; (c) fuller applicability of Banking Regulations Act, 1949 to cooperative banks; (d) steps to strengthen PACS; (e) promoting SHGs as cooperatives within cooperatives of short-term structure; (f) reforming deposit insurance as per recommendations of RBI committee of 1999;

---

[4] RBI, July 1, 2008 notification 'Master Circular—Lending to Priority Sector'.

(g) selective de-layering of co-operative credit system; (h) integration of long-term and short-term structures; and (i) relaxation of norms for refinance support to cooperatives. The Vaidyanathan Committee's (2005) thrust is that Cooperative Credit Societies need (a) special financial assistance to wipe out accumulated losses and strengthen its capital base; (b) institutional restructuring to make for democratic, member driven, autonomous and self-reliant institutions; (c) radical changes in the legal framework to empower the RBI to take direct actions and to the extent deemed appropriate for prudent financial management of banks, and (d) qualitative improvement in personnel in all tiers and at all levels through capacity building and other interventions, leading to an increase in overall efficiency.

The latest committee under the Chairmanship of A.V. Sardesai revisited the issue of restructuring the RRBs (Sardesai Committee, 2005). It held that 'to improve the operational viability of RRBs and take advantage of the economies of scale, the route of merger/amalgamation of RRBs may be considered taking into account the views of the various stakeholders'.

Khan Committee (2005) recommended promotion of Banking Facilitator (BF) and Banking Correspondence (BC) as an agent of banks for reaching the banking services to the unreached. On MFIs, the Khan committee while on one hand did not favor loan pricing and left it to the market force to decide the fair price, on the other way, had suggested keeping watch on lending rates of MFIs to protect customer interest. Accepting the committee's recommendation, RBI started pushing the SCBs for extending banking facility through BF and BC.

Apart from appointing high level rural credit committees to examine and get rid of the weaknesses of credit delivery mechanism support, subsidy flows and loan waivers were also in forefront. The Government of India in Union Budget—2006–07 also announced to provide Short Term Credit to Farmers at the interest rate of 7% p.a. with an upper limit of ₹ 3,00,000 on the principal amount with interest subvention of 2% p.a. to the banks. The same incentive continued for 2007–08 also. Government has further approved interest subvention of 3% (instead of 2%) for the year 2008–09.

In his budget for the year 2008–09, the then Union Finance Minister, P. Chidambaram, announced a complete waiver of all farm loans, that became overdue on December 31, 2007, and which remained unpaid till February 27, 2008, taken by three crore marginal and one crore small farmers, for implementation by all scheduled commercial banks, besides

RRBs and co-operative credit institutions (including Urban Cooperative banks) and Local Area Banks. The amount eligible for debt waiver or debt relief, as the case may be, comprised of (a) in the case of a short-term production loan, the amount of such loan (together with applicable interest) and (b) in case of investment loan, the installments of such loan that are overdue (together with applicable interest on such installments).

The scheme covered entire waiver of 'eligible amount' in the case of a small or marginal farmer, while, One Time Settlement (OTS) in the case of 'other farmers' (operating on land more than 2 hectares), where the farmer will be given a rebate of 25 per cent of the 'eligible amount' subject to the condition that the farmer pays the balance of 75 per cent of the 'eligible amount'. In the case of a farmer who has obtained investment credit for allied activities where the principal loan amount does not exceed ₹ 50,000, he would be classified as "small and marginal farmer" and, where the principal amount exceeds ₹ 50,000, he would be classified as 'other farmer', irrespective in both cases of the size of the land holding, if any[5].

Though the move of loan waiver has been welcomed on the backdrop of the government effort toward unleashing the mounting debt burden of the farming community, it has attracted various criticisms on grounds that it would act as a disincentive for healthy financial behavior and that the scheme is somewhat regressive and skewed in favor of irrigated big farmers (Dev, 2008)[6].

1.3 A REVIEW OF INFORMAL SECTOR CREDIT

Several studies on informal sector credit (see Bardhan and Rudra (1978)[7], Timberg and Aiyar (1984)[8], Ghate (1988)[9], Iqbal (1988)[10],

---

[5]For detailed information regarding the scheme also refer to the RBI notification RPCD. No. PLFS.BC.72/05.04.02/2007-08 dated May 23, 2008.

[6]Dev, S.M. (2008). Agriculture: Absence of a Big Push. *Economic and Political Weekly*, 43(15), 33–39.

[7]Bardhan, P.K. and Rudra, A. (1978). Interlinkage of Land, Labour and Credit Relations: An Analysis of Village Survey Data in East India. *Economic and Political Weekly*, 13(6/7), 367–384.

[8]Timberg, T.A. and Aiyar, C.V. (1984). 'Informal Credit Markets in India', Economic Development and Cultural Change, Vol. 33, No. 1, pp. 43–59.

[9]Ghate, P.B. (1988). "Informal Credit Markets in Asian Developing Countries", *Asian Development Review*, Vol. 6, No. 1, pp. 64–85.

[10]Iqbal, F. (1988). The Determinants of Moneylender Interest Rates: Evidence from Rural India. *Journal of Development Studies*, 24(3), 364–78.

Dasgupta (1989)[11], Bell (1990)[12], Sarap (1991)[13], Swaminathan (1991)[14], Datta (1992)[15], Bhaumik and Rahim (1999)[16], Mahajan and Ramola (2003)[17], Basu (2005)[18], Reddy (2007)[19] and others) have examined various aspects of informal financial sector. Stylized features of rural credit market which evolve from these studies are as follows:

1. Even after sixty years of systematic efforts, formal financial sources could not make serious dent in the operation of its informal counterpart even while offering loan at a much lower price.
2. Both lender and borrower seem to face considerably lower transaction cost in informal finance sector in comparison to formal setting.
3. Restriction of formal sector loan mostly for productive purposes has made poor peasants dependent on informal sources for fulfilling most of their consumption and contingency needs.
4. Wide variability in pricing in informal sector across target groups seems to depend on 'profit potential' of the loanee, quality of collateral, caste, loan size, purpose of borrowing, elasticity of loan demand as well as length of relationship.
5. Credit layering evolves as a common practice where upstream agents, both formal and informal, lend to local informal downstream agents like traders and large farmers to relend the sum to scattered small borrowers.

---

[11] Dasgupta, *et al.* (1989). Report on Informal Credit Markets in India: Summary, *National Institute of Public Finance and Policy*, New Delhi.

[12] Bell, C. (1990). Interactions between Institutional and Informal Credit Agencies in Rural India. *World Bank Economic Review*, 4(3), 297–327.

[13] Sarap, K. (1991). Interlinked Agrarian Markets in Rural India. New Delhi: Sage Publications.

[14] Swaminathan, M. (1991). Segmentation, Collateral Undervaluation and the Rate of Interest in Agrarian Credit Markets: Some Evidence from Two Villages in South India. *Cambridge Journal of Economics,* 15(2), 161–178.

[15] Datta, S.K. (1992). Understanding Rural Moneylenders—A Study of Two Villages from West Bengal. Study sponsored by NABARD. Ahmedabad: Indian Institute of Management.

[16] Bhaumik, S.K. and Rahim, A. (1999). Interlinked Credit Transactions in Rural West Bengal. *Indian Journal of Agricultural Economics*, 54(2), 169–184.

[17] Mahajan, V. and Ramola, B.G. (2003). Financial Services for the Rural Poor and Women in India: Access and Sustainability. Background paper prepared for the World Bank. Washington D.C.: World Bank.

[18] Basu, Priya (2005). A Financial System for India's Poor. Economic and Political Weekly, September 10, 4008–4012.

[19] Reddy, S.T.S. (2007). Diary of a Moneylender. Economic and Political Weekly, July 21, 3037–3043.

6. High incidence of interlinkage between credit and other markets is a rule, rather than an exception in informal sector.

Over the last two decades, a set of semiformal financial institutions, known as microfinance institutions (MFIs) have come up that are in touch with local community and can obtain information about loanee at a cost lower than its formal counterpart. Two broad approaches characterize the microfinance sector in India—groups formed by NGOs/Government agencies and linked to banks to ensure safe savings and required flow of credit (Self Help Group Bank Linkage Program—SBLP) and Non-Banking Financial Companies (NBFCs) form groups and perform financial intermediation role as a lender to groups after sourcing loans from banks, other financial institutions (MFI Bank Linkage Model). They employ self selection of group members and joint liability as screening and monitoring mechanism (Besley and Coate, 1995)[20]. Peer pressure acts as collateral substitute in this arrangement (Morduch, 1999)[21]. Regular transaction ensures close monitoring of the loan. Even within the formal sector, lending to group instead to individual has been suggested as a measure to increase the size of entitlement set of the applicant acceptable to formal financial agency (Basu, 1997)[22].

Besides ensuring wider presence of formal financial channel, government also tried to rein in the operation of moneylenders. The Constitution of India has conferred the power to legislate on matters relating to money-lending and moneylenders to the states. Most of them have enacted the laws. Provisions of such legislations are requirement of obtaining license to carry moneylending business, ceiling on interest rate, transparency in operation, penalty for carrying business without license.

The All India Debt and Investment Survey as on June 30, 2002 (NSSO, 2003) highlighted an alarming increase of the dependence on informal sector credit sources. The survey highlighted that informal agencies provided 42.3 per cent of the outstanding loans of rural households in 2002 as against 30.6 per cent in 1991–92 (Table 1.3). The share of moneylenders in total dues increased from 17.5 per cent in 1991 to 25.7 per cent in 2002 (NSSO, 1998 and 2005).

---

[20]Besley, T. and Coate, S. (1995). Group Lending, Repayment Incentives and Social Collateral. *Journal of Development Economics,* 46, 1–18.

[21]Morduch, J. (1999). The Microfinance Promise. *Journal of Economic Literature*, 37 (December), 1569–1614.

[22]Basu, S. (1997). Why Institutional Credit Agencies are Reluctant to Lend to the Rural Poor: A Theoretical Analysis of the Indian Rural Credit Market. *World Development*, 25(2), 267–280.

Table 1.3: Sources of Credit in Rural India

	Source of Credit	*1951*	*1961*	*1971*	*1981*	*1991*	*2002*
A.	**Non-Institutional**	**91.2**	**84.0**	**68.3**	**36.8**	**30.6**	**42.3**
	1. Money lenders	68.6	62.0	36.1	16.1	17.5	25.7
	2. Traders	5.0	7.2	8.4	3.2	2.2	5.2
	3. Relatives/Friends	14.4	6.4	13.1	8.7	4.6	8.5
	4. Landlords/Others	3.2	8.4	10.7	8.8	6.3	2.9
B.	**Institutional**	**8.8**	**15.8**	**31.7**	**63.2**	**66.3**	**57.7**
	1. Government etc.	3.1	5.5	7.1	3.9	5.7	2.5
	2. Cooperative Society	4.8	9.7	22.0	29.8	23.6	19.6
	3. Commercial banks	0.9	0.6	2.4	26.6	35.2	35.6
	4. Others	–	–	0.2	0.7	1.8	–
C.	**Unspecified**	–	**0.2**	–	–	**3.1**	–
		100.00	100.00	100.00	100.00	100.00	100.00

Source: All India Rural Credit Survey for 1951. All India Debt and Investment Survey for other years.

In this context, RBI formed a technical group for review of legislations on moneylending (2006). The major recommendations of the group were, (i) simplifying the registration (renewal) process of moneylenders, (ii) ceiling on interest rate by state governments, (iii) keeping trade credit out of the purview of proposed legislation, (iv) including agricultural input dealers who provide input on credit within the purview of proposed legislation, (v) existing moneylenders, input dealers, agricultural traders, commission agents, agricultural output processors, vehicle dealers, oil/petrol dealers, or any other person with localized knowledge may be appointed by institutional lenders as *accredited loan providers* for on-lending to a large number of excluded masses.

Further during 2006, RBI launched the National Rural Financial Inclusion Plan (NRFIP) to reach financial service as no-frill savings account, small overdraft facility, micro-insurance to at least 50 per cent of the excluded population by 2012.

Our brief review of the literature on informal credit in India would remain incomplete without reference to the Malegam Committee. Although micro-finance companies were experiencing rapid growth since 2000, in retrospect it turned out to be a bubble, which burst out in the citadel of micro-finance companies—namely, in the state of Andhra Pradesh, when a crisis of confidence cropped up following several allegations of rampant profiteering, coercive collection of loan repayment and resulting suicides of borrowers, and the state government came up with a stringent Andhra Pradesh Micro Finance Institutions (Regulation of Money Lending) Act. On the heels of this micro-finance crisis of Andhra Pradesh, the Reserve Bank of India set up a Sub-Committee of its Central Board of Capital 'to study the issues and concerns in micro-finance sector, under the Chairmanship of Shri Y.H. Malegam' in October 2010. After a careful examination of the contentious management issues in the sphere of micro-finance provided by 'for profit' institutions—namely, (i) Identity crisis as these organizations had no legal status; (ii) charging of usurious interest rates coupled with rampant profiteering; (iii) multiple lending and over indebtedness of clients; (iv) non-transparent charges of various kinds, for which poor borrowers had no clues; and (v) coercive repayment collection practices, the Malegam Committee recommended creation of a separate category—designated as NBFC-MFIs and defined as 'a company which provides financial services predominantly to low-income borrowers, with loans of small amounts, for short-terms on unsecured basis, mainly for income generated activities, with repayment schedules which are more frequent than those normally stipulated by commercial banks'.

The Malegam Committee also recommended several additional qualifications for these companies like that they will hold not less than 90% of its total assets in the form of qualifying assets, that individual loans can be disbursed to a single borrower up to ₹ 25,000, subject to a maximum annual family income of ₹ 50,000, and that not less than 75% of the loans should be for income generating purposes. Another important restrictive recommendation is of an average 'margin-cap' of 10% for MFIs with loan portfolio of ₹ 100 crore and more, and of 12% for smaller MFIs. It also imposed an interest cap of 24% on individual loans, besides stipulating that interest charge can only comprise of three components—namely, processing fee, interest rate and insurance charge, to achieve transparency. It also made a number of recommendations to mitigate the problems of multiple lending, over-borrowing, ghost borrowers and coercive methods of recovery, including a minimum period of moratorium between disbursement of a loan and its recovery, and establishment of a Credit Bureau, a Customer Protection Code, grievance redress procedures and ombudsman, and a specified Code of Corporate Governance. It proposed a four-wheeler regulatory approach with the responsibility to be shared by MFIs, industry associations, banks and the RBI. It also recommended that NBFC MFIs under the proposed Micro-Finance (Development and Regulation) Bill 2010 should not allow them to do business of providing first service, but they may be exempted from the State Money Lending Acts. It is a very healthy sign that this Committee while recognizing the need for protection of borrowers has also recognized the need to maintain recovery culture as well as free flow of funds in the system, in the interest of the borrowers themselves. The RBI has come up with several stipulations, while broadly accepting the recommendations of the Malegam Committee[23]. The Central Government however seems to be following a wait and see policy before it converts the proposed Micro-Finance Bill of 2010 into an Act.

1.4 MINIMALIST CREDIT VERSUS CREDIT PLUS APPROACH

Over the years, the economy is becoming more specialized, dynamic and complex, while, on one hand, services required for supporting livelihoods have become more diverse, and on the other, it has become necessary to have more specialized service provider. This also needs the agents to be cost effective to make things available to ultimate consumer at lowest possible price. Datta, *et al.* (2004) suggested that aforementioned issue could be addressed by creation of collaborative arrangements. For supporting livelihoods, services are required in input supply, output marketing, infrastructure, technology development, research and training institutes and extension agents among others. In today's economy, one agency cannot develop competency of providing all of them. Thus, an input supply company needs to collaborate with an output marketing company, which in turn needs to collaborate with a credit provider, and so on, which the authors termed as to build a collaborative polygon as they noted that collaboration among aforesaid six prime service providers is essential for livelihood promotion of rural households.

The credit plus approach is one such holistic intervention founded on the observation that "credit cannot stand alone[24]". Several institutions in India have been attempting to put this approach into practice by attempting to intervene in several markets simultaneously (along with credit), with varying scale, scope and degrees of success. Table 1.4 prepares a preliminary typology of the credit plus interventions that are being practiced in India today.

---

[23] *Source:* http://www.rbi.org.in/scripts/BSPressReleaseDisplay.aspx?prid=23780 accessed on 30/09/2012.

[24] A phrase due to Pan A. Yotopoulos.

At the bottom of the credit plus pyramid, we have Self-Help Groups (SHGs) promoted by traditional MFIs that focus on savings and credit as well as providing some training to members on running successful businesses. At a higher level we see some SHGs that are part of the SHG-bank-NGO linkage scheme which goes, beyond credit, in terms of both provision of technical inputs, training etc., and federating the SHGs in order to tap scale economies in input and consumer good supply and/or in output marketing. Consumer supply is an important intervention in the plus approach since it represents efforts on the part of institutions to increase member and domain centrality[25] and hence increase the likelihood that the intervention will be sustainable.

The next level of pyramid has new generation livelihood promotion organizations like BASIX that expand the credit plus ambit to include in depth technical training as well as local value addition services, a more complete suite of financial services including insurance and commodity derivatives training as well as formation of producer organizations.

At the apex of the pyramid we have multipurpose cooperative societies such as Cooperative Rural Bank and Marketing Society, Mulukanoor (MCRB) and the Amalsad Vibhag Vividh Karyakari Sahakari Khedut Mandali, Amalsad (AVVKSKM) that provide credit, savings, insurance, input supply, output marketing, technical assistance, and consumer supplies with a sharp commodity focus. Given the above hierarchal structure of the credit plus approach, it can be observed that moving up the ladder implies that one is moving away from the partial equilibrium approach and entering into a multi-market general equilibrium framework.

1.5 BROAD OBJECTIVES

Given the above-stated background about the status of credit in India as well as the emerging concept of Credit Plus Approach, the broad objectives of this research study are set up as follows:

1. To find out whether all segments of the rural economy interested in credit (including allied agricultural activities) are really getting access to credit, and whether credit is being efficiently delivered to them in

---

[25] Shah, *et al.* (1992) have suggested 'member-centrality' as the importance of the co-operative in the economies of its members and 'domain-centrality' as the prominence and centrality of the cooperative in the economy of its domain. Seeking Salience: Governance and Management in Indian Village Cooperatives, Institute of Rural Management, Anand.

right quantity and quality, and at appropriate terms and conditions, which they can afford.

2. To ascertain whether the terms and conditions of credit are consistent with the prevailing norms of equity i.e., whether government interventions and regulations are sound enough to get rid of imperfections in the market for credit.
3. To determine whether available credit is being complemented by necessary extension services either from government extension agencies or, directly from credit agencies so as to contribute to livelihood promotion of borrowers across farm and non-farm activities and sustainability of both borrowers and lenders.
4. To assess whether government policy of cheap and concessional credit including loan waivers are contributing to efficiency, equity and sustainability of credit for rural households i.e., to what extent govt. policy of the last several years has contributed to the first three objectives of this study.
5. To suggest a road map in terms of policy measures and innovative schemes to remove the gaps in existing credit policy and regulations, so as to strengthen the first three objectives of credit.

1.6 CONCEPTUAL AND METHODOLOGICAL FRAMEWORK

Clearly a strong theoretical and conceptual framework (as depicted in Table 1.5) lies behind the above-stated objectives. For example, the issue of 'efficiency' underlying the first objective must address not only availability of credit in right quantity i.e., in adequate amount to the borrower, but also its availability in right quality i.e., available at the right time and with minimum response time depending upon the borrower purpose. Credit must also be available to the borrower at appropriate terms and conditions which he can afford. Terms and conditions of credit cover a whole spectrum of price and price-like parameters such as interest rate, the mode of interest charging, repayment schedule, borrower's transaction cost, borrower's collateral demanded, and flexibility in supply and repayment of credit etc. If and only if the borrower gets loan at terms and conditions favorable to what he can afford, there can be borrower surplus, akin to the concept of consumer surplus, which is a reward for participation in a reasonably good market for credit. It is therefore important to judge through both objective and subjective analysis of different sections of borrowers whether and to what extent they enjoy borrower surplus, and whether government policy interventions are really helping them enjoy a reasonable surplus. Since the market for credit is very much prone to the problems of market failure due to adverse selection (of both borrower and lender), moral hazard (i.e., willful or induced default) and hold up problem (i.e., non-willful default due to multiple risks beyond control of either the borrower or the lender), it is pertinent to examine whether and to what extent the process of credit delivery and credit repayment conforms to the safeguards against the various reasons for market failure, and whether government regulations and interventions have helped overcome these problems. In fact, the terms and conditions of credit must also cover the lenders' cost of credit include-ing various risks confronted and subsumed by the lender. No organization of credit can survive unless it earns at least a normal rate of profit within its credit operations. Thus, the issue of efficiency of credit delivery must address all these multifarious issues.

On the issue of equitable distribution of the benefits of credit, the pertinent question is whether the gains from credit, i.e., borrower's surplus and lender's surplus (in the language of market economics) are fairly distributed between the two sides. In this context, the theoretical grounding is provided by the first and second fundamental theorems of welfare economics. The first theorem asserts that a perfectly competitive market for credit would always maximize the sum total of borrower and lender surplus, thus leading to Pareto efficiency. The issue is therefore whether or not the market for credit is close to a competitive one or not, and if not, whether government interventions and regulatory framework has contributed to competitiveness of credit market. The justification for government intervention and regulations flow from the second fundamental theorem of economics which asserts that under appropriate corrective measures a suitable distribution of benefits of credit between borrower and lender can be achieved. The issue is whether or not government interventions and regulatory framework have been able to reduce the extent of imperfection in credit market. This can be checked by attempting to measure Learner's measure of the degree of monopoly power $L = (P-MC)/P$, i.e., to what extent the price charged by a lending institution to its immediate client is above the marginal cost of credit. Marginal cost of credit can be decomposed into cost of borrowing (i.e., line of credit) and operational cost. Through suitable comparison of alternatives, one can even try to measure social cost of credit to differentiate between actual cost inclusive of subsidies and its opportunity cost. Naturally, both quantitative and qualitative analysis of a selective group of lending institution is necessary to fulfill these objectives[26].

On the issue of sustainability of credit operations, it is extremely important to see whether the prevailing systems of credit delivery and repayment are able to set up a Coasian process (thanks to famous Coase Theorem)—namely, (i) a suitable property right system across borrowers, lenders and other stakeholders, (ii) minimum transaction cost and (iii) no wealth effect, to lead to value maximization. Especially important in this context is to find out whether and to what extent the institutions of credit are able to empower borrowers and particularly vulnerable sections of rural borrowers to put control of their future growth and development in their own hands.

As mentioned earlier, the justification for government intervention and regulations flow from two fundamental theorems of welfare economics, and also from Coase Theorem. Through critical analysis of various lending institutions it is necessary to see the implications of rapid expansion of formal credit facilities, interest rate reductions, innovative credit schemes, innovative sectoral credit schemes and occasional loan waiver policy for efficiency, equity, sustainability and socio-economic impact of credit operations.

1.7 ORGANIZATION OF STUDY REPORT

The present study is organized in nine chapters. Chapter 1 covers the background, review of rural credit market, minimalist Credit versus Credit Plus approach, objectives and conceptual and methodological framework. Chapter 2 deals with the coverage and sampling design, description of the study area and sample borrowers. Chapter 3 deals with access to credit. Chapter 4 describes terms and conditions of various credit contracts. Chapter 5 highlights borrowers' pre as well as post-contractual transaction costs involved in credit contracts across sources. Chapter 6 deals with interlinked credit transactions and credit plus approach. Chapter 7 brings out the nature and extent of extension service available from government extension agency or, credit plus provider. Chapter 8 covers the implications of latest debt waiver and debt relief scheme. Chapter 9 concludes the study, with summary and policy recommendations.

---

[26] Unfortunately, almost all lending units failed to entertain our request for requisite lending side data, though attempts are still being made to undertake a few qualitative case studies on lending organizations in the consolidated all-India report.

Table 1.4: The Credit Plus Pyramid

Tier	*Organisations*	*Credit Plus Elements*				
		Other Financial Services	*Input and Output Market Activities*	*Technical Assistance*	*Consumer Supplies*	*Collective Action Services*
1.	Multi purpose PACS like Mulukanoor and Amalsad	Savings Insurance (accident)	Input supply and output marketing	Productivity enhancement Local value addition	Yes	Potentially yes, by virtue of being a coop
2.	New-generation MFIs like BASIX	Savings Insurance (life, health, rainfall, crop) Commodity derivatives	Input and output linkages	Productivity enhancement Local value addition	No	Yes, by virtue of forming producer orgs
3.	Bank-SHG-NGO linkage	Savings	Some	Some	Some	Yes, by virtue of being a SHG
4.	MFIs like SHARE, Sanghamitra	Savings	No	Some	No	Yes, by virtue of forming SHGs

Table 1.5: Methodological Apparatus for the Study

Objective/ Goal	*Issues*	*Conceptual Framework*	*Implies*
Efficiency	(a) Whether credit been made available to the borrower in a.1. Right quantity—adequate amount; a.2. Right quality—timeliness and minimum response time as per purpose; a.3. Right terms and conditions—spectrum of price and price like parameters including interest rate, repayment schedule, transaction cost, collateral, flexibility etc. (b) If these are favorable as compared to what borrower is willing to offer for credit such that there exists borrower/consumer surplus. Need to judge the same both subjectively and objectively. (c) Whether terms and conditions are taking care of adverse selection, moral hazard (willful default), asset specificity (hold up, i.e., non-willful default).	First fundamental theorem of welfare economics[27]	Perfectly competitive market; Pareto efficiency; Maximum Producer and consumer surplus.

Table contd...

[27] "There are two fundamental theorems of welfare economics. The first states that any competitive equilibrium or Walrasian equilibrium leads to a Pareto efficient allocation of resources. The second states the converse, that any efficient allocation

Table 1.5 contd...

Objective/ Goal	*Issues*	*Conceptual Framework*	*Implies*
	(d) Whether the terms and conditions of credit: 1. Covering lender's cost of credit including risk. 2. Providing 'normal' profit to credit operations.		
Equity	(a) Whether distribution of surplus consistent with prevailing norms of equity. (b) Check extent of imperfection in credit market by attempting to measure degree of monopoly power i.e. L = (P-MC)/P where, P is price charged by lending institution to its immediate clients, MC is marginal cost of credit (decomposition of operational cost and social cost is necessary).	Second fundamental theorem of welfare economics.	Through appropriate redistributive measure, a suitable Pareto efficient solution can be arrived under usual assumptions.
Sustain-ability	Whether the available credit is leading to the following: (a) Whether productive asset been created leading to recurring benefit to borrower. (b) Whether human capital been formed. (c) Whether credit supported activities are environmentally sustainable. (d) Whether borrower and lender interactions adequately empower borrowers, in particular, to put control in their hands.	Whether Coasian process[28] set in motion—namely, a suitable property right system, minimum transaction cost and no wealth effect.	

Table contd...

can be sustainable by a competitive equilibrium. Despite the apparent symmetry of the two theorems, in fact the first theorem is much more general than the second, requiring far weaker assumptions.

The first theorem is often taken to be an analytical confirmation of Adam Smith's "invisible hand" hypothesis, namely that competitive markets tend toward an efficient allocation of resources. The theorem supports a case for non-intervention in ideal conditions: let the markets do the work and the outcome will be Pareto efficient.

The second theorem states that out of all possible Pareto-efficient outcomes, one can achieve any particular one by enacting a lump-sum wealth redistribution and then letting the market take over. This appears to make the case that intervention has a legitimate place in policy—redistributions can allow us to select from all efficient outcomes for one that has other desired features, such as distributional equity".

Source: http://en.wikipedia.org/wiki/Fundamental_theorems_of_welfare_economics

[28] "In law and economics, the Coase theorem, attributed to Nobel Prize laureate Ronald Coase, describes the economic efficiency of an economic allocation or outcome in the presence of externalities. The theorem states that if trade in an externality is possible and there are no transaction costs, bargaining will lead to an efficient outcome regardless of the initial allocation of property rights. In practice, obstacles to bargaining or poorly defined property rights can prevent Coasian bargaining".

Source: http://en.wikipedia.org/wiki/Coase_theorem

Table 1.5 contd...

Objective/ Goal	*Issues*	*Conceptual Framework*	*Implies*
Impact of government intervention	(a) Expansion of formal credit facilities. (b) Interest rate subvention. (c) Innovation in credit supply including innovative schemes. (d) Occasional loan waiver.	Whether wealth effect created/avoided for socially and economically vulnerable sections of the society.	

CHAPTER 2

Coverage, Sampling Design, Description of Study Area and Characteristics of Sample Borrowers

2.1 COVERAGE AND SAMPLING DESIGN

Based on collective decisions taken at the behest of the Ministry of Agriculture, Govt. of India in two meetings in February 11, 2010 and June 19, 2010, respectively, the study is proposed to be undertaken in several states with the help of several AER Centers, whereas IIM, Ahmedabad will, besides coordinating the study, will undertake primary data collection primarily in two states of Chhattisgarh and West Bengal. Given rather low order of penetration of Micro-Finance Institutions (MFIs) in the country or a state as a whole, but presence of clusters of such organizations, a cluster of MFIs is chosen from each of these states in the first place, before selecting 3–5 villages from that cluster such that all forms of credit organizations—both formal (namely, Scheduled Commercial Banks (SCBs), RRBs, Primary Agricultural Credit Societies (PACS) or multipurpose PACS, branches of District Central Cooperative Banks (DCCBs)) and non-formal (namely, traditional money-lending organizations, and MFIs—whether promoted by government, NGO or NABARD as non-profit entities, or promoted by private bodies for profit-making (called NBFCs[1])) are functioning side by side in those villages to test contestability across various lending organizations.

---

[1]It is important to distinguish between two categories of NBFCs, in view of their emphasis on credit-plus activities. Whereas BASIX seems to have a strong credit-plus bias, the other NBFC MFIs are mostly following 'minimalist credit' policy. So, in order to have a strong focus on credit versus credit-plus approaches, it is necessary to select villages where BASIX and multipurpose PACS are functioning, alongside SCBs/RRBs/PACS and non-BASIX type MFIs. Since only formal credit institutions (SCBs/RRBs/Coops) are entitled to offer benefits of loan waiver or relief, it is also necessary to ensure existence of these formal credit institutions

Once a cluster of 3–5 villages within a single agro-climatic region of a state is selected, at the same time ensuring functioning of all types of formal and non-formal lending institutions, the next step is to canvass three different types of questionnaires for these villages: (i) a village questionnaire to identify and record village level demographic, land use, infrastructure, and government (schematic) intervention parameters, which may have an impact on credit delivery and credit use; (ii) lender-level questionnaire to seek some broad information from 2 or 3 major lending organizations[2] within each selected village on their business and experience on loan waiver/relief; and (iii) a questionnaire to perform complete enumeration of all village households[3] on the basis of some of their credit experiences both before March 2007 (the cut-off date for loan waiver/relief scheme) and after March 2008 (the announcement date for the above-mentioned scheme), so that a suitable stratified sample of borrower households together with suitable controls can be drawn during the last stage of data collection.

Assuming an average of five villages from each state, 20 sample farmer households from agriculture and allied activities, and another five from non-farm sector are drawn per village on the basis of probability proportionate stratified random sampling. Two criteria are judiciously used for purpose of stratification: (i) source of borrowing—broadly whether formal or non-formal; and (ii) the landholding class of the borrower—whether landless, small or large. Obviously, within the category of formal sector borrowers, we encounter households benefiting or not benefiting from loan waiver/relief scheme. At the same time, another control of five households per village is drawn using stratified random sampling principle to represent households, who didn't apply for loan or didn't get a loan prior to March 2007 (though they had

within the 3–4 selected villages. These villages, moreover, must belong to a common agro-climatic region within a state.

[2] Obviously, these questionnaires can be canvassed to only formal sector credit institutions—SCBs, RRBs and Coops., though all of them may not respond quickly or may not respond at all. Given our understanding with BASIX, we may be able to procure some information from local BASIX field offices. We have assured organizations that all such information are to be preserved as confidential and not to be used for any purpose other than this research project of the Ministry of Agriculture.

[3] If a village is too large in terms of number of households, some representative hamlets of that village (not exceeding 300 households) are used for complete enumeration. In that case, only those households covered under complete enumeration will constitute the population from which the sample (both treatment and control) will be drawn.

asked for). So, assuming a total sample of 30 households from each village and five villages from each state, there will be 30 × 5 = 150 households per state. For the current IIMA study two states—West Bengal and Chhattisgarh are chosen. Five and three villages are chosen, respectively, through the above stated process. Only a single village with well-functioning multipurpose PACS in Gujarat is chosen, pending choice of the rest of the villages from Gujarat by the relevant AER centre, to highlight the importance of most well-functioning multipurpose PACS. Thus, the total size of sample households turns out to 350 for this IIMA study.

Collected data is expected to highlight the distinctive characteristics of households not availing credit, those starved of credit, those accessing only non-formal credit, and those getting formal credit with or without loan waiver/relief benefits, besides highlighting differential credit experiences of different borrower groups. Although one-point data is no good for impact assessment or for sustainability analysis in the true senses of these terms, nevertheless some preliminary or tentative findings can be highlighted for more rigorous testing in the future—preferably with help of a panel type data. Data analysis will use not merely statistical tables but also linear hierarchal regression model to highlight the role of various exogenous parameters at household level, at village level, at lending institution level and also at broad policy level for the country as a whole.

2.2 BROAD FEATURES OF STUDY VILLAGES

Table 2.1 reveals that in terms of total number of households, all the selected villages or village hamlets are medium-sized ones. But there lies considerable variation in distribution of landholding across them. The incidence of landless household is very high in Tarpongi, Bhatagaon and Amalsad, moderately high in Metiyakhali and relatively less in other five villages. Dhusnikhali and Khulna are dominated by small farmers, with a share of around 99%. While in Chorabidya, Madhusudankati and Kendri the corresponding figure ranges within 85–95%, for rest it hovers within 51–73%. The incidence of large farmer households is highest in Kendri (16%) followed by Amalsad (14%). The wide variation in household across diverse operational landholding categories in selected villages ensures an appropriate setting to study the impact of accessibility to credit on livelihood promotion.

Table 2.1: Distribution of Households (HH) by Landholding Status across Sample Villages

	Village Name	*Contestability among Prominent Credit Sources*	*No. of Landless HH*	*No. of Small Farmer HH*	*No. of Large Farmer HH*	*Total*
1.	Dhuchnikhali Dist: 24 Pgs (N), West Bengal	RRB, PACS, SHG	0 (0.00)	178 (99.44)	1 (0.56)	179
2.	Chorabidya Dist: 24 Pgs (S), West Bengal	SCB, MFI, NBFC-MFI	17 (13.18)	110 (85.27)	2 (1.55)	129
3.	Khulna Dist: 24 Pgs (N), West Bengal	RRB, PACS, SHG	1 (0.40)	243 (98.78)	2 (0.82)	246
4.	Metiyakhali Dist: 24 Pgs (N), West Bengal	MPACS, SCB, NBFC-MFI	51 (26.70)	144 (64.29)	1 (0.45)	196
5.	Madhusudankati Dist: 24 Pgs (N), West Bengal	SCB, MPACS	0 (0.00)	127 (94.49)	6 (5.51)	133
6.	Kendri Dist: Raipur, Chhattisgargh	RRB, PACS, SHG	7 (3.66)	153 (80.10)	31 (16.3)	191
7.	Tarpongi Dist: Simgaon, Chattisgargh	RRB, MPACS, NBFC-MFI	73 (32.59)	132 (58.93)	19 (8.48)	224
8.	Bhatagaon Dist: Raipur, Chhattisgargh	SCB, MFI, PACS	77 (37.74)	119 (58.33)	8 (3.92)	204
9.	Kotha Dist: Navsari, Gujarat	SCB, MPACS	65 (34.76)	96 (51.34)	26 (13.90)	187

Note: Landless households: Nil landholding; small farmer households: > 0 to = < 2 ha; large farmer household: > 2 ha. MPAC = multipurpose PACS.

Table 2.2 indicates primary activity wise distribution of households across sample villages. Farming is the primary activity for seven out of the nine sample villages. Though in Dhuchnikhali farming is the primary activity for majority of the households, fishery as allied activity is followed by around one-fourth of the households. At Metiyakhali, fishery is the primary activity. At Kendri, in most cases farming is the secondary activity while service/trade has emerged as the primary activity.

Table 2.2: Primary Activity-wise Distribution of Households across Sample Villages

Village Name	*Farming*	*Allied*	*Other*	*Total*
Dhuchnikhali	121 (67.60)	50 (27.93)	8 (4.47)	179
Chorabidya	108 (83.72)	8 (6.20)	13 (10.08)	129
Khulna	186 (75.61)	28 (11.38)	32 (13.01)	246
Metiyakhali	5 (2.55)	114 (58.16)	77 (39.29)	196
Madhusudankati	117 (87.97)	0 (0.00)	16 (12.03)	133
Kendri	11 (5.70)	0 (0.00)	180 (94.3)	191
Tarpongi	154 (68.75)	1 (0.45)	69 (30.80)	224
Bhatagaon	126 (61.76)	2 (0.98)	76 (37.25)	204
Kotha	120 (64.17)	5 (2.67)	62 (33.16)	187

Note: Figures in parentheses represent % of households across various activities.

Table 2.3: Literacy Rates across Selected Villages

	Village Name	*Literacy Rate %*
1.	Dhuchnikhali	60
2.	Chorabidya	50
3.	Khulna	60
4.	Metiyakhali	30
5.	Madhusudankati	70
6.	Kendri	50
7.	Tarpongi	40
8.	Bhatagaon	50
9.	Kotha	80

Table 2.3 highlights that Kotha, the single village selected from Gujarat, has the highest literacy rate (80 %) followed by Madhusudankati (70 %), a village from West Bengal. Except two villages—namely, Tarpongi (40 %) and Metiyakhali (30 %) literacy rate in rest five villages range within 50–60 %.

In terms of household's breakup along caste and religion lines, only Chorabidya, a village from West Bengal, is dominated by Muslim community. Dhuchnikhali, Khulna, Metiyakhali (all three from West Bengal) and Kendri (from Chhattisgarh) has more households from Hindu SC/ST/OBC community.

Table 2.4: Caste and Religious Break-up of Households across Selected Villages

	Village Name	*% of Hindu Households*		*% of Minority Households*
		Upper Caste	*SC/ST/OBC*	
1.	Dhuchnikhali	8	90	2
2.	Chorabidya	10	20	70
3.	Khulna	5	95	0
4.	Metiyakhali	20	80	0
5.	Madhusudankati	40	50	10
6.	Kendri	30	60	10
7.	Tarpongi	75	20	5
8.	Bhatagaon	60	30	10
9.	Kotha	40	50	10

As it can be observed from Table 2.5, all sample villages from West Bengal and one village (i.e., Tarpongi) from Chhattisgarh have more than 95 % land under agriculture. The corresponding figure for the rest three villages ranges within 76–79 %.

Table 2.5: Broad Land Use Pattern across Selected Villages

	Village Name	*% of Agricultural Land in Use*	*% of Current and Permanent Fallow Land*	*% of Common Property Land*	*% of Land Under Cultivable Waste*
1.	Dhuchnikhali	100.00	0.00	0.00	0.00
2.	Chorabidya	100.00	0.00	0.00	0.00
3.	Khulna	96.76	0.00	1.88	1.37
4.	Metiyakhali	100.00	0.00	0.00	0.00
5.	Madhusudankati	100.00	0.00	0.00	0.00
6.	Kendri	75.93	0.00	23.23	0.84
7.	Tarpongi	97.77	0.00	1.49	0.74
8.	Bhatagaon	76.89	7.30	2.43	13.38
9.	Kotha	78.43	14.01	2.80	4.76

Incidence of irrigation which has a direct effect on off-take of agricultural finance varies quite a lot across the sample villages (Table 2.6). In contrast to Metiyakhali and Kotha (villages from West Bengal and Gujarat, respectively) which has more than 90% agricultural land under assured irrigation, access to such facility is limited to less than 10% of cultivable land in Dhuchnikhali, Chorabidya, Khulna (villages from West Bengal) and Tarpongi (village from Chhattisgarh). For rest of the villages, it is fairly high and ranges within 75–84%. It is relevant to note these contrasting features of the sample villages as these are likely to influence the access to credit, which is being dealt in the chapters, which follow.

Table 2.6: Percentage Distribution of Agricultural Land by Irrigational Status across Selected Villages

Village Name	*Under Assured Irrigation*	*Under Non-Assured Irrigation*	*Under No Irrigation (rainfed)*
Dhuchnikhali	9.46	8.24	82.30
Chorabidya	8.11	40.54	51.35
Khulna	2.94	47.06	50.00
Metiyakhali	90.00	10.00	0.00
Madhusudankati	83.33	16.67	15.30
Kendri	75.12	9.59	15.30
Tarpongi	7.62	2.86	89.52
Bhatagaon	84.18	15.82	0.00
Kotha	96.43	3.57	0.00

Table 2.7: Distance in Kilometres of Selected Infrastructure Facilities from the Selected Villages

	Dhuchnikhali	*Chorabidya*	*Khulna*	*Metiyakhali*	*Madhu-sudankati*	*Kendri*	*Tarpongi*	*Bhatagaon*	*Kotha*
Agri Extension	6	10	5	4	2	0	0	0	3
Agri-input retailer	0	0	3	4	2	0	15	1	3
APMC sub-yard	20	0	20	25	2	5	15	2	3
Bus route	8	0.5	8	0	0	0	0	1	1
Cable TV	0	13	0	0	0	0	0	0	0
Cinema/theatre	15	13	38	23	2	22	15	4	4
Commercial bank	17	15	15	4	2	5	15	1	4
Cooperative	0	13	0	1	0	0	0	1	4
Drinking water	0	0	0	0	0	0	0	0	0

Table contd...

Table 2.7 contd...

	Dhuchnikhali	*Chorabidya*	*Khulna*	*Metiyakhali*	*Madhu-sudankati*	*Kendri*	*Tarpongi*	*Bhatagaon*	*Kotha*
Fair price shop	20	5	15	4	2	0	0	1	4
Farm machinery provider	20	65	38	4	2	5	30	1	3
Farm machinery repair	20	65	10	21	2	5	0	1	3
Farmers' club	0	0	3	4	0	0	15	0	0
Girls' secondary school	6	13	5	4	1	5	15	1	2
Higher secondary school	15	5	0	4	1	5	0	1	2
Highway	60	65	18	22	2	0	0	1	6
ITI College	60	20	45	70	1	5	15	5	15
Medical store	0	7	0	4	2	5	0	0	0
MFI (govt.)	10	0	15	21	2	23	30	5	20
NBFC branch	5	5	15	4	2	5	30	6	20
Nearest town	45	13	37	21	0	15	15	0	15
Panchayat	0	1.5	0	0	2	0	0	0	0
Petrol pump/fuel	8	11	6	4	2	5	15	2	4
PHC/hospital	6	7	0	3	2	0	0	5	4
Police station	6	13	5	14	2	5	10	5	6
Post office	0	1	3	4	1	0	0	1	0
Primary school	0	0	0	0	0	0	0	0	0
Provision store	20	13	20	4	2	0	0	1	4
Pucca road	0	0	0	0	0	0	0	0	0
Railway station	40	13	35	20	0	0	12	12	1
Regular market	0	0	0	4	2	5	0	0	3
RRB branch	1	10	0	4.5	2	5	0	2	2
Secondary school	5	5	0	4	1	0	0	1	2
Telephone facility	0	1	0	0	0	0	0	0	0
Veterinary doctor	6	13	5	2	0	0	0	0	0
Village haat	0	5	0	0	2	0	0	0	3
Youth club	5	0	0	0	2	0	15	0	0

Note: Zero indicates that the facility is available inside the village.

The infrastructure position of selected villages is depicted in Table 2.7, which shows the minimum distance of important facilities from these villages. Although there observed to be a wide variation among the villages, it is seen in general that Dhuchnikhali and Chorabidya, two villages from West Bengal are comparatively weak in terms of infrastructure facilities in comparison to other seven selected villages.

CHAPTER 3

Access to Sources of Credit

3.1 INTRODUCTION

The purpose of this chapter is to analyze rural household's access to various sources of credit based on their past experiences as well as their actual experiences during 2009–10. As mentioned earlier, the various sources of credit are classified into three broad classes—formal, semi-formal and informal. Formal sources are again categorized into two—formal 1, which includes scheduled government or private commercial banks and RRBs, and formal 2 including all types of co-operative banks—namely, PACS, multi-purpose PACS and their higher-tier bodies. Similarly semi-formal source has two components, the first referring to MFIs promoted by government/NABARD/NGOs, whereas the second refers to only those MFIs, which are promoted by private NBFCs. Informal sources of credit are divided into two categories—the first includes only traditional money lenders, as commonly understood, whereas the second includes all other informal lenders like friends, relatives, traders, merchants, grocery shopkeepers, medical shops etc.

The rural households are asked questions regarding their access to the above—stated sources of credit-first, which sources they can access for credit, given their past experiences during 2009–10. The concept of access is defined in gross and net terms. For example, if a household has potential access to schedule government commercial banks, private commercial banks as well as RRBs, then the household is looked upon as having 3-fold access to formal 1 source in gross terms, though in net terms the access is only 1.

This chapter is organized as follows. In the following section we shall analyze access to credit across sources as well as across sample of villages. The next section would attempt to relate access thus defined to various attributes of borrower households. The last section summarizes the stylized findings of this chapter.

3.2 POTENTIAL AND ACTUAL ACCESS ACROSS CREDIT SOURCES AND ACROSS VILLAGE SCENARIOS

Tables 3.1 and 3.2A to 3.2I analyze notions of access vis-à-vis the different sources of credit as well as across different study villages. Table 3.1 reports

Table 3.1: Indices of Access to Credit of all Sample Borrowers across Sources during 2009–10 (n = 350)

(1)	*(2)*	*(3)*	*(4)*
Sources of Credit[1]	*Access in Actual Sense in Numbers*[2]	*% Importance of Different Actual Sources*	*Gross Actual Access as Proportion of Net Actual Access*[3]
Formal 1	43 (56)	9.7 (9.5)	1.3
Formal 2	142 (195)	32.1 (32.9)	1.4
Semi-formal 1	51 (56)	11.5 (9.5)	1.1
Semi-formal 2	22 (22)	5.0 (3.7)	1.0
Informal 1	62 (62)	14.0 (10.5)	1.0
Informal 2	123 (201)	27.8 (34.0)	1.6
Total	**443 (592)**	**100 (100)**	**1.3**

Note: Figures in parentheses represent gross figures as defined in footnote 2.

[1] Formal 1 includes scheduled government or private commercial banks and RRBs, whereas formal 2 includes all types of cooperative banks—whether PACS or multipurpose PACS or their higher-tier bodies. Semi-formal 1 refers to MFIs promoted by government/NABARD/NGOs, whereas semi-formal 2 refers to only MFIs promoted by private NBFCs. Informal 1 stands for moneylenders as readily understood by the borrower, though the notion of traditional moneylenders seems to have undergone sea changes, given the usual derogatory connotation assigned to this term. Informal 2 includes all other informal lenders including friends, relatives, traders, merchants, grocery shopkeeper, medical shop etc.

[2] In gross calculation access to multiple sources within the same category (e.g., to commercial banks and RRBs) is counted as many times as there is access, whereas in actual counting access to any of these sources is counted as unity, irrespective of multiple access.

[3] A value larger than unity means the borrower has access to multiple sources or multiple access to the any of the sources within the same category. These ratios are calculated in terms of actual figures in column (4). These figures are generated by expressing corresponding numbers within brackets in column (2) as a ratio to the number in the same column outside brackets.

all the sample households' access in actual term (with distinction between gross and net access) in column 2 of this table. Column 3 shows percentage importance of these various sources of credit actual sense. The last column (i.e., column 4) displays gross access figures as the ratio of the corresponding net access figures for the notion of potential and actual access respectively. Figures in the last column therefore indicate whether or not the household has multiple accesses within the same credit source.

From column 3 in Table 3.1 it is seen that formal 2 has the highest importance as source of credit in actual sense. Informal 2 has got the second highest importance. Formal 1 has lower order of importance (holding fifth position in column 3, respectively). Semi-formal 1 and semi-formal 2 have still lower order of importance. In overall terms, the formal credit sector has overall 41.8 % weightage in terms of actual access, whereas 16.5 %[4] and 41.8 % weightage goes to semi-formal and informal source of credit, respectively, based on the sample households' actual experiences during 2009–10. These broad results highlight the basic dilemma of rural credit—namely, that our formal sources, in spite of their best efforts, cannot capture more than 41.8 % of rural credit, whereas informal sources remain equally important with another 41.8 % share, while the fast-growing semi-formal sector captures another 16.5 % of the rural clientele. As it is seen in column 4, the entire sample of 350 households has on average 1.3 units of loan across sectors. This Figure is 1.6 for informal 2 and 1.4 for formal 2, while this figure is 1.3 and 1.1, respectively, for formal 1 and semi-formal 1. Interestingly, semi-formal 2 and informal 1 have provided only 1 unit of loan per borrower (i.e. no multiple loans to these households).

Tables 3.2A to table 3.2I depict the picture of access to credit by sample borrowers in each of the nine villages in the sample. In other words, these tables provide us a picture of how the rural borrower' access to credit is undergoing variation as we move from one village scenario to another. Table 3.2A shows the picture for the village of Bhatagaon, which is located in closed proximity to the state capital of Raipur of Chhattisgarh state. Because of its close proximity to a city area and the presence of an NGO active in formation of SHGs among farmers and linking them to formal sources of credit, the overall importance of formal sector credit is 42.3 % in actual terms (column 3). While informal 1 has no share in actual terms, informal 2 has 15.4 % share, while semi-formal sources capture another 42.3 % credit. In other words, inspite of

[4]That the MFI sector has captured 16.5 % share of rural credit seems to indicate potency of this segment.

the close proximity to the state capital and its strong urbanization effect, the village of Bhatagaon has not been able to increase the share of formal sector credit beyond 42.3 %.

Table 3.2A: Indices of Access to Credit Sources of Sample Borrowers of Bhatagaon during 2009–10 (n = 50)

(1)	*(2)*	*(3)*	*(4)*
Sources of Credit	*Access in Actual Sense in Numbers*	*% Importance of Different Actual Sources*	*Gross Actual Access as Proportion of Net Actual Access*
Formal 1	0 (0)	0.0 (0.0)	0.0
Formal 2	11 (11)	42.3 (39.3)	1.0
Semi-formal 1	10 (12)	38.5 (42.9)	1.2
Semi-formal 2	1 (1)	3.8 (3.6)	1.0
Informal 1	0 (0)	0.0 (0.0)	0.0
Informal 2	4 (4)	15.4 (14.3)	1.0
Total	**26** **(28.0)**	**100** **(100)**	**1.1**

Note: Figures in parentheses represent gross figures as defined in footnote 2.

The picture is slightly different in the village of Kendri, another village of Chhattisgarh, which is located slightly far off from the state headquarter of Raipur. Here the formal sector has a share of 64.2 %, semi-formal has no share, but informal has 35.8 % share (Table 3.2B, column 3).

Table 3.2C displays the picture for the village of Tarpongi in Chhattisgarh state which is located about 60 km from the state capital of Raipur. Tarpongi has a good banking network due to presence of an RRB, multi-purpose PACS and functioning of BASIX's loan network. Here formal sector has provided actual access to 56.0 % of sample borrowers, whereas the weights of semi-formal and informal sectors are 26.0 % and 18.0 %, respectively. In other words, semi-formal sources have played a vital role in Tarpongi in restricting the importance of the informal sector to an order of 18.0 % only.

Table 3.2B: Indices of Access to Credit Sources of Sample Borrowers of Kendri during 2009–10 (n = 50)

(1)	*(2)*	*(3)*	*(4)*
Sources of Credit	*Access in Actual Sense in Numbers*	*% Importance of Different Actual Sources*	*Gross Actual Access as Proportion of Net Actual Access*
Formal 1	1 (2)	1.5 (2.9)	2.0
Formal 2	42 (42)	62.7 (60.7)	1.0
Semi-formal 1	0 (0)	0.0 (0.0)	0
Semi-formal 2	0 (0)	0.0 (0.0)	0
Informal 1	12 (12)	17.9 (17.1)	1.0
Informal 2	14 (12)	17.9 (20.0)	1.2
Total	**67 (70.0)**	**100 (100)**	**1.0**

Note: Figures in parentheses represent gross figures as defined in footnote 2.

Table 3.2C: Indices of Access to Credit Sources of Sample Borrowers of Tarpongi during 2009–10 (n = 50)

(1)	*(2)*	*(3)*	*(4)*
Sources of Credit	*Access in Actual Sense in Numbers*	*% Importance of Different Actual Sources*	*Gross Actual Access as Proportion of Net Actual Access*
Formal 1	0 (0)	0.0 (0.0)	0
Formal 2	28 (28)	56.0 (53.0)	1.0
Semi-formal 1	3 (3)	6.0 (5.8)	1.0
Semi-formal 2	10 (10)	20.0 (19.2)	1.0
Informal 1	4 (4)	8.0 (7.7)	1.0
Informal 2	5 (7)	10.0 (13.5)	1.4
Total	**50 (52.0)**	**100 (100)**	**1.0**

Note: Figures in parentheses represent gross figures as defined in footnote 2.

The pictures of five West Bengal villages are captured in tables 3.2D to 3.2H. In the village of Choravidya in Sunderbans area of West Bengal (Table 3.2D), cooperatives are weak; but there is a scheduled government commercial bank, besides a fairly good network of a private NBFC called Bandhan. In terms of actual access, formal sector has provided access to the order of 12.3 %, whereas semi-formal and informal sectors have shares of 27.7% and 60.0%, respectively. In this scenario, while the semi-formal sector is taking care of a significant part of borrower's demand, the slender coverage of formal sector credit makes this area highly dependent on informal sector credit (60.0%).

Table 3.2D: Indices of Access to Credit Sources of Sample Borrowers of Choravidya during 2009–10 (n = 30)

(1)	*(2)*	*(3)*	*(4)*
Sources of Credit	*Access in Actual Sense in Numbers*	*% Importance of Different Actual Sources*	*Gross Actual Access as Proportion of Net Actual Access*
Formal 1	7 (7)	10.8 (8.3)	2.0
Formal 2	1 (1)	1.5 (1.2)	1.0
Semi-formal 1	8 (8)	12.3 (9.5)	1.0
Semi-formal 2	10 (10)	15.4 (11.9)	1.0
Informal 1	12 (12)	18.5 (14.3)	1.0
Informal 2	27 (46)	41.5 (54.8)	1.7
Total	**65** **(84)**	**100** **(100)**	**1.3**

Note: Figures in parentheses represent gross figures as defined in footnote 2.

The story of Dhushnikhali from Sunderbans area of West Bengal (Table 3.2E) is similar to that of Choravidya—the formal sector has a marginal existence with only 8.6% coverage. Although the semi-formal sector has a fairly good coverage of 32.8%, thanks to the functioning of an NGO-promoted SHGs, the dependency on informal source of credit is very high (about 58.6%), as can be seen from column 5 of Table 3.2E.

In the village of Khulna (Table 3.2F) there is a cooperative bank, besides NGO-promoted SHGs, although the latter are less powerful than in the village of Dhushnikhali. As a result, the actual coverage of formal sector credit is of the order of 31.4%, while the same for semi-formal and informal sectors are 19.6% and 47.0%, respectively.

Table 3.2E: Indices of Access to Credit Sources of Sample Borrowers of Dhusnikhali during 2009–10 (n = 30)

(1)	*(2)*	*(3)*	*(4)*
Sources of Credit	*Access in Actual Sense in Numbers*	*% Importance of Different Actual Sources*	*Gross Actual Access as Proportion of Net Actual Access*
Formal 1	5 (9)	8.6 (12.3)	1.8
Formal 2	0 (0)	0.0 (0.0)	–
Semi-formal 1	19 (22)	32.8 (30.1)	1.2
Semi-formal 2	0 (0)	0 (0)	–
Informal 1	13 (13)	22.4 (17.8)	1.0
Informal 2	21 (29)	36.2 (39.7)	1.4
Total	**58** **(73)**	**100** **(100)**	**1.3**

Note: Figures in parentheses represent gross figures as defined in footnote 2.

Table 3.2F: Indices of Access to Credit Sources of Sample Borrowers of Khulna during 2009–10 (n = 30)

(1)	*(2)*	*(3)*	*(4)*
Sources of Credit	*Access in Actual Sense in Numbers*	*% Importance of Different Actual Sources*	*Gross Actual Access as Proportion of Net Actual Access*
Formal 1	0 (0)	0.0 (0.0)	–
Formal 2	16 (16)	31.4 (28.1)	1.0
Semi-formal 1	9 (9)	17.6 (15.8)	1.0
Semi-formal 2	1 (1)	2.0 (1.8)	1.0
Informal 1	12 (12)	23.5 (21.1)	1.0
Informal 2	12 (30)	23.5 (45.6)	2.2
Total	**65** **(84)**	**100** **(100)**	**1.3**

Note: Figures in parentheses represent gross figures as defined in footnote 2.

The village of Madhusudankati (Table 3.2G) has a well-known Multi-purpose PACS, which has a coverage of 57.8 % in terms of actual access. However, as semi-formal sources are practically non-existent, informal source of credit still has large percentage coverage—namely, of the order of 42.2 %. In other words, the dominance of a well functioning cooperative could not sufficiently reduce the clientele share of informal credit sources. Probably semi-formal sources have a scope for penetration and take away a section of informal sector customers. The story is very similar in the village of Metiyakhali, where there is a fairly well-functioning LAMPS (Table 3.2H). Its share in terms of actual access is of the order of 26.7 %. Together with commercial banking sectors, the formal credit sector has coverage of nearly 50.0 %. However, the slender clientele size (3.4 %) of semi-formal sources makes the borrowers of this village dependent on informal sources to the extent of 46.5 %.

Table 3.2G: Indices of Access to Credit Sources of Sample Borrowers of Madhusudankati during 2009–10 (n = 30)

(1)	*(2)*	*(3)*	*(4)*
Sources of Credit	*Access in Actual Sense in Numbers*	*% Importance of Different Actual Sources*	*Gross Actual Access as Proportion of Net Actual Access*
Formal 1	0 (0)	0.0 (0.00)	0.0
Formal 2	26 (26)	57.8 (55.32)	1.0
Semi-formal 1	0 (0)	0.0 (0.00)	0.0
Semi-formal 2	0 (0)	0.0 (0.00)	0.0
Informal 1	3 (3)	6.7 (6.38)	1.0
Informal 2	18 (18)	35.6 (38.30)	1.0
Total	**45** **(47)**	**100** **(100)**	**1.0**

Note: Figures in parentheses represent gross figures as defined in footnote 2.

The village of Kotha under a national award winning multi-purpose PACS called Amalsad provides a very interesting picture in Table 3.2I. Although some semi-formal and informal sources have existence in terms of potential access, in terms of actual access during 2009–10, this multi-purpose PACS has clientele size of 84.0 %, while the rest 16.0 % is captured by formal 1 source i.e., by the commercial banking sector. The

Table 3.2H: Indices of Access to Credit Sources of Sample Borrowers of Metiyakhali during 2009–10 (n = 30)

(1)	*(2)*	*(3)*	*(4)*
Sources of Credit	*Access in Actual Sense in Numbers*	*% Importance of Different Actual Sources*	*Gross Actual Access as Proportion of Net Actual Access*
Formal 1	13 (23)	22.4 (28.4)	1.8
Formal 2	16 (18)	27.6 (22.2)	1.1
Semi-formal 1	0 (0)	0 (0)	–
Semi-formal 2	2 (2)	3.4 (2.5)	1.0
Informal 1	6 (6)	10.3 (7.4)	1.0
Informal 2	21 (31)	36.2 (39.5)	1.5
Total	**58 (81)**	**100 (100)**	**1.4**

Note: Figures in parentheses represent gross figures as defined in footnote 2.

Table 3.2I: Indices of Access to Credit Sources of Sample Borrowers of Kotha during 2009–10 (n = 50)

(1)	*(2)*	*(3)*	*(4)*
Sources of Credit	*Access in Actual Sense in Numbers*	*% Importance of Different Actual Sources*	*Gross Actual Access as Proportion of Net Actual Access*
Formal 1	8 (15)	16.0 (5.7)	1.9
Formal 2	42 (53)	84.0 (20.2)	1.3
Semi-formal 1	0 (0)	0.0 (0.0)	0.0
Semi-formal 2	0 (0)	0.0 (0.0)	0.0
Informal 1	0 (0)	0.0 (0.0)	0.0
Informal 2	0 (0)	0.0 (0.0)	0.0
Total	**50 (68)**	**100 (100)**	**1.4**

Note: Figures in parentheses represent gross figures as defined in footnote 2.

average number of loans per borrower is 1.4, the corresponding figures for the commercial banking sector and the cooperative bank being 1.9 and 1.3, respectively.

3.3 POTENTIAL AND ACTUAL ACCESS RELATED TO SELECTED BORROWER ATTRIBUTES

In this section, an attempt is made to relate different borrower attributes to the indices of access as developed in the preceding paragraphs. The different attributes of borrowing households considered here are his caste and religion, his poverty status, agricultural land holding, level of education and borrowing status. Tables 3.3 to 3.7 perform this analysis.

Table 3.3: Access of Borrowers to Credit Classified by Caste and Religion

(1)	*(2)*		
Sources of Credit	*Actual Access*		
	Upper Caste	*SC/ST/OBC*	*Minority*
n = 350	**97 (28)**	**237 (67)**	**16 (5)**
Formal 1	10 (18)	43 (78)	2 (4)
Formal 2	59 (30)	134 (69)	1 (1)
Semi-formal 1	7 (13)	46 (82)	3 (5)
Semi-formal 2	12 (55)	4 (18)	6 (27)
Informal 1	12 (19)	44 (71)	6 (10)
Informal 2	28 (14)	146 (73)	27 (13)

Note: Figures in parentheses indicate percentages of row total for columns (2) and (3).

Table 3.3 reports the observed number of access in actual sense during 2009–10. These indicators of access are tabulated separately for three broad categories of borrowers—upper caste, SC/ST/OBC and minority—all across the six separate sources of credit. The figures in parentheses within each row indicate percentages of row total across each sub-group (demarcated by column 2). The total number of borrower households are spread across the three caste and religion categories in percentage terms as 28, 67 and 5. If the observed percentages of households having access to any of the credit sources is found to be different from their overall percentage in the total sample, these differences are noted and suitably interpreted in the paragraphs which follow. In terms of actual access, upper caste Hindu seem to have performed better only in two sources—namely, formal 2 and semi-formal 2. The SC/ST/OBC category of borrowers seems to have enjoyed this edge with respect to all sources except semi-formal 2. The minority class of borrowers has better actual access in semi-formal 2 and both sources of informal credit.

Table 3.4 relates credit access to borrower's poverty status—namely, whether BPL or APL borrowers have better access to any of the existing sources of credit. As this table brings out, in terms of actual access, BPL borrowers seem to have edges in almost all credit sources, except cooperatives. The APL households enjoy better access only with respect to formal 2 source.

Table 3.4: Access of Borrowers to Credit Classified by their Poverty Status

(1)	*(2)*	
Source	*Actual Access 2009–10*	
	BPL	*APL*
n = 350	**184 (53)**	**166 (47)**
Formal 1	34 (62)	21 (38)
Formal 2	94 (48)	101 (52)
Semi-formal 1	40 (71)	16 (29)
Semi-formal 2	15 (68)	7 (32)
Informal 1	45 (73)	17 (27)
Informal 2	136 (68)	65 (32)

Note: Figure in parentheses indicate percentages of row total.

Table 3.5 relates borrowers' agricultural land holding status to actual access. The landless households enjoy some edge in terms of actual access in both formal 1 and informal 2 sectors. The small farmer category of borrowers seems to have advantages in accessing credit in all the sectors except formal1 and semi-formal 2. Large farming households' advantages persist in terms of actual access only for formal 2 and semi-formal 2 sectors.

Table 3.5: Access of Borrowers to Credit Classified by their Agricultural Landholding Status

(1)	*(2)*		
Source	*Actual Access 2009–10*		
	Landless	*Small Farmer*	*Large Farmer*
n = 350	**33 (9)**	**274 (78)**	**43 (13)**
Formal 1	8 (15)	40 (73)	7 (13)
Formal 2	6 (3)	154 (79)	35 (18)
Semi-formal 1	4 (7)	51 (91)	1 (2)
Semi-formal 2	6 (8)	12 (55)	4 (18)
Informal 1	5 (8)	53 (85)	4 (6)
Informal 2	21 (10)	164 (82)	16 (8)

Note: Figures in parentheses indicate percentages of row total.

As Table 3.6 displays, illiterate borrowers enjoy better access in actual terms also in formal 1 and informal 2 segments. Literate households have better access not only in semi-formal 1 segment but also in both the segments of informal credit. In fact, they have also enjoyed better actual access in informal 1 segment. Educated borrowers are found to have better access in formal 2, semi-formal 2 and informal 1 segments. Highly educated borrowers have better access to both types of formal lending sources.

Table 3.7 is analyzing access by relating it to individual household's borrowing status during 2007–08. In terms of the sampling household's borrowing status, they are classified into five categories—those who did not get any loan from any source, those who did not apply for any loan, those who got formal loan and also a loan waiver, those who got formal loan but no loan waiver, and finally, those who are exclusively informal sector borrowers. The first category, who did not get loan from any source, seems to have better access to not only informal sources, but also in semi-formal 1. Those households who didn't apply for loan during 2007–08 seem to have better access not only with respect to informal 2 sources, but also with respect to at least formal 2 sources. The two groups of formal sector borrowers (irrespective of whether they have got the benefit of loan waiver or not) seem to have better access not only in both formal sources, but also to both informal sources, and at least to semi-formal 1 source. The last category of exclusively informal borrowers has better access only with respect to informal and semi-formal sources.

3.4 STYLIZED FINDINGS ON ACCESS TO CREDIT

A description of access of borrowers in actual sense to various sources of credit across several state scenarios seem to bring out the following stylized facts:

- When the cooperative banking structure is very powerful, it tends to severely restrict the operation of all other sources of credit, as it has happened in case of the Kotha village under Amalsad cooperative society of South Gujarat.
- The commercial banking sector inclusive of RRBs (i.e., formal 1 source) has generally a marginal role, very rarely exceeding 10.0 % coverage in terms of catering to the demands of actual loanees. True, the formal 1 sector has provided multiple loans per loanee, but their capacity to convert borrowers' expectations into actual supply of loan is rather meager.
- The fact that the importance of traditional moneylenders in terms of providing access is about 14 % on average among the total sample, and sometimes it is as high as 24 %, as in the context of Khulna village, speaks volumes for the resilience of this segment of lenders, on the one hand, and also for the failure of our formal loan sources, on the other.
- The most spectacular source of credit is informal 2 covering a host of local lenders—friends, relatives, contractual parties, local shopkeepers, etc. Except in the village of Kotha under Amalsad Cooperative Society, where the services of these informal sources seem to have been successfully replicated by this cooperative organization, this source has on average 28 % claim among actual loanees in the total sample, while having a maximum share of nearly 42 % in the interior village of Choravidya near Indian Sunderbans. An important feature of this source is that it can provide easy access, not only by providing assurance as a potential supplier, but also through converting such assurances into realities at a very high rate. This source has also the capability to produce multiple loans per loanee.
- The share of the informal source seems to have been restricted to some extent when not only formal sources, especially cooperatives, are functioning well, but also the intermediate sector, which we call semi-formal sources, is in existence and providing good competition. Very often this role of MFIs—not only those promoted by government/

NABARD/NGOs, but also those promoted by private NBFCs like BASIX, as in the context of village Tarpongi in Chhattisgarh are not appreciated enough in policy making circles.

Table 3.6: Access of Borrowers to Credit Classified by Maximum Level of Education among Adult Household Members

(1)	*(2)*			
Source	*Actual Access 2009–10*			
	Illiterate	*Literate*	*Educated*	*Highly Educated*
n = 350	**27 (8)**	**96 (27)**	**144 (41)**	**83 (24)**
Formal 1	6 (11)	20 (37)	11 (20)	17 (31)
Formal 2	4 (2)	32 (16)	100 (52)	58 (30)
Semi-formal 1	5 (9)	23 (41)	18 (32)	10 (18)
Semi-formal 2	1 (5)	4 (20)	13 (65)	2 (10)
Informal 1	4 (6)	24 (39)	29 (47)	5 (8)
Informal 2	21 (11)	79 (40)	80 (40)	20 (10)

Note: Figure in parentheses indicate percentages of row total; Literate = just literate, who knows the three R's; Educated = Above secondary; Highly educated = Above graduation.

When we relate household attribute to their experiences of loan access to several lending categories, we observe the following stylized features:

- Upper caste Hindu borrowers seem to have enjoyed better loan access in formal 2, i.e., the cooperative sector. Minority group borrowers seem to have enjoyed better actual access in all semi-formal and informal sources but not in formal sectors.
- BPL categories of borrowers seem to have enjoyed better access to loans in almost all sources except in cooperatives (i.e., formal 2). APL category households, on the other hand, seem to have better access in cooperatives (i.e., formal 2).
- Although the landless categories of borrowers have got some better access to formal 1 loan sources, they have been mostly dependent on informal 2 source for loans. The small holdings of borrowers have managed to enjoy better access not only in informal sources

Table 3.7: Access of Borrowers to Credit Classified by their Borrowing Status in 2007–08

(1)	*(2)*				
Source	*Actual Access 2009–10*				
	1	*2*	*3*	*4*	*5*
n= 350	**15 (4)**	**46 (13)**	**46 (13)**	**201 (58)**	**42 (12)**
Formal 1	0 (0)	6 (12)	11 (22)	32 (65)	6 (11)
Formal 2	1 (1)	26 (14)	28 (15)	136 (71)	4 (2)
Semi-formal 1	3 (9)	3 (9)	6 (18)	22 (65)	22 (42)
Semi-formal 2	0 (0)	2 (11)	2 (11)	15 (79)	3 (14)
Informal 1	3 (6)	6 (11)	10 (19)	34 (64)	9 (15)
Informal 2	10 (6)	24 (15)	29 (18)	102 (62)	36 (19)

Note: Figure in parentheses indicate percentages of row total; 1 = Did not get loan, 2 = Did not apply for loan, 3 = Had access to formal source and enjoyed loan waiver benefit; 4 = Had access to formal source, but didn't get loan waiver benefit; 5 = Had access exclusively to informal source.

but also in cooperatives and semi-formal 1 source. Elite capture of cooperatives is again obvious when one observes the better access to cooperative credit of large holding.

- It appears that by virtue of policy thrust illiterate and just literate borrower households have managed to get better actual access to formal 1 source. Educated and highly-educated categories of borrowers (and especially the latter) seem to have better access to both types of formal sources, and especially to cooperatives. Informal 2 sources seem to have helped provide access to all types of borrowers.
- Individual households who didn't get loan during 2007–08 are mostly dependent on informal and semi-formal 1 sources. Those households who didn't apply for loan during 2007–08 turned out to be mostly dependent on formal and informal 2 sources in 2009–10. Households who could access formal loans in 2007–08 are dependent on not only formal sources but also on other sources, namely, semi-formal 1 and both informal sources. Households borrowing exclusively from informal sources are mostly dependent on semi-formal and informal sources of credit.

CHAPTER 4

Terms and Conditions of Rural Credit

4.1 INTRODUCTION

Credit being a package of services provided and repaid over a period of time has multifarious attributes beyond merely its quantity and price—namely, the interest rate. Nor is it a standard package of services, so that its attributes vary over time and space as per the demands of the borrower and supply interests of its lender. In the rural context of a developing country like India, naturally one needs to understand variations in the multifarious attributes of credit, besides bringing out the stylized patterns therein, if rural credit has to be placed on a strong conceptual foundation for policy making. This is what is being attempted in the present chapter.

This chapter is organized as follows. The next section highlights the basic quantitative attributes of loans across sources. Section 3 brings out the different attributes of interest rates observed in the rural context. Section 4 talks of loan purposes. Section 5 highlights the various types of collaterals being used by borrowers to access loans, besides bringing out the incidence of loan cases where the borrowers' hold deposits with the loan sources. Section 6 describes the terms and conditions of loan repayment. Section 7 examines the extent of loan default together with their cited reasons. Section 8 describes the common recourses generally available to borrowers in cases of non-willful default. The final section summarizes the findings besides concluding this chapter.

4.2 BASIC QUANTITATIVE ATTRIBUTES OF LOANS

Table 4.1 summarizes the basic quantitative attributes of 582 loan cases, which are found among 350 sample households during 2009–10. Of these 582 loans, only 33 arose out of the formal commercial banking sector and RRBs (i.e., formal-1). 200 loan cases arose in the cooperative sector. SHGs promoted by government/NABARD/NGOs gave rise to 63 loan cases, whereas NBFC-promoted MFIs generated only 20 loan cases. The traditional rural moneylenders, as understood by the villagers, generated 50 loan cases, whereas the largest number of loan cases (216) came from the other rural lending agencies like friends, relatives, traders, merchants, shopkeepers etc., whom we have referred to as informal-2 in our presentation. The statistical significance of the various loan sources becomes obvious from the fact that 37.11% loan cases arose from informal-2 source, followed by 34.36% share of formal-2, i.e., the co-operative sector. These two are the most dominant sources of credit as observed among sample borrowers during 2009–10. The informal moneylenders (informal-1) and SHGs formed by government/NABARD/NGOs (i.e., semiformal-1) have shares of 8.50% and 10.82%, respectively. The formal commercial banking sectors and RRBs, in spite of policy emphasis on this segment, captures only 5.67% share, whereas NBFC-promoted MFIs, in spite of hue and cry over this segment, has a meager share of 3.43%. It must be remembered in this context that these relative shares arose in spite of the fact that two pockets of MFIs were deliberately

Table 4.1: Basic Quantitative Attributes of Loans across Loan Sources (6 categories)

Loan Source	*Years of Familiarity*	*Loan Amount in ₹*	*Kind Component in %*	*Duration in Months*	*Estimated Reducing Balance Annualized Interest Rate (%)*
Informal-2 (216)	11.95	7231.48	75.56	11.4	23.92 (0.0–41.70)
Informal-1 (50)	9.66	10060	8.6	10.02	54.87 (19.90–61.00)
Semi-formal-2 (20)	3.2	11550	0	13.4	26.85 (26.10–27.60)
Semi-formal-1 (63)	5.98	5230.16	5.95	9.35	10.80 (10.50–11.0)
Formal-2 (200)	10.64	25751.5	50.37	11.27	6.23 (3.0–12.0)
Formal-1 (33)	5.91	81409.09	3.03	20.67	9.14 (6.90–19.90)

Note: Figures in parentheses represent numbers of loan cases arising out of the sample households.

chosen from the states of Chhattisgarh and West Bengal. In other words, in spite of deliberate choice of pockets where MFIs have been functioning, they (i.e., semi-formal-1 and semi-formal-2) could not cover more than 14% loan cases. Their importance would be much less in terms of loan share, as these sources provide relatively small loans.

In terms of years of familiarity with these loan sources, it is found that informal-2 source has the longest years of familiarity (11.35 years) followed by cooperatives (i.e., formal-2) (10.64) and traditional money-lenders, i.e., informal-1 (9.66). Semi-formal-1 and formal-1 have lesser years of familiarity (5.98 and 5.91, respectively). NBFC-promoted MFIs (i.e., semi-formal 2) have the least years of familiarity with the borrowers, because of their more recent origin. In other words, among the various loan sources, both informal sources and the cooperative sector have the longest years of association with the rural borrowers. This fact needs to be kept in mind while talking of rural credit policy. In other words, the vast experiences of these sources cannot be taken lightly while framing any useful policy towards rural credit.

As it can be seen from column 3 of Table 4.1, formal-1 source has provided the largest loan amount (nearly ₹ 81,000 on average), followed by formal-2 (more than ₹ 25,000), semi-formal-2 (slightly more than ₹ 11,500), informal-2 (₹ 10,000) and informal-1 (₹ 7,200), whereas semi-formal-1 provides the lowest-sized loan (₹ 5,200). So, it is natural to believe that for large loans, there is hardly any substitute for formal-1 source. Apparently, this is also to the liking of formal-1 source for transaction cost reasons. Cooperatives, on the other hand seem to have developed a niche for supplying medium-sized loans. Among the other sources, there seems to be much more competition in supply of small to medium-sized loans.

Column 4 of Table 4.1 provides the kind components of loan amount arising from various sources. Informal-2 (i.e., other rural lenders) and formal-2 (i.e., cooperatives), not only because of their proximity and closeness to borrower, but also sometimes because of the nature of their own activities (e.g., supplying inputs, groceries, medicines etc., or marketing of produce), are in a strong position to provide a fairly large component of loan in kind. Informal-1 (i.e., traditional rural money-lenders) and semi-formal-1 (i.e., SHGs promoted by government/ NABARD/NGOs), too, are sometimes in a position to provide a component of the loan in kind, though it is rather insignificant (not more than 6% on average). Formal-1 and semi-formal-2 lenders are simply incapable of supplying loan in kind. Thus, only some sources, because of the nature of their operations and locational advantages, have comparative advantages in supplying a part of the loan in kind, taking advantage of complementarities between credit and a few pertinent services the borrower needs for effective use of credit—a point which is sometimes lost sight of in policy discussion pertaining to credit.

In terms of average duration of loans (column 5 of Table 4.1), the situation is fairly comparable, though the commercial banking segment and RRBs seem to have provided longest-duration loans on average (20.67 months), followed by NBFC-promoted MFIs, other rural lenders, cooperatives, traditional moneylenders and government/NABARD/NGO-promoted MFIs (13.40, 11.40, 11.27, 10.02 and 9.35 months, respectively). In this context, the comparable strengths of NBFCs, the cooperatives and the two forms of informal lenders deserve special attention for purpose of future discussion on policy matters in this context.

Column 6 of Table 4.1 has reported the average annual interest rates charged by different sources together with their minimum and maximum values. Since the duration of loan varies across sectors, we don't have an alternative other than expressing and comparing interest figures on annual basis, but this type of comparison may be quite misleading when an urgent loan given say, for half a day to a trader-borrower by a lender even say at 1% interest rate may end up producing too exorbitant an annual figure of 730%! Actually, interest rates can't be compared unless and until the loan cycle, which again varies with the borrower's production or consumption cycle, is also taken into consideration. So, the comparison we are performing here is at best an imperfect one. In terms of annual average figures, as calculated and reported here, interest rates of both formal sources, semi-formal-1 and even informal-2 sources are somewhat comparable, though the rate is least for cooperatives, and second-least for commercial banks and RRBs. The estimated annual figure is the highest for traditional moneylenders (55%), as expected. As comparing only average annual rates across sources has its limitations, in the section which follows, we shall pursue the interest rate story a little further, bringing out the various dimensions of interest rate calculations.

4.3 IMPORTANT DIMENSIONS BEHIND INTEREST RATE CALCULATIONS

Table 4.2A brings out the basis for interest rate calculations, as understood and revealed by the borrowers. The basis could be daily, monthly, yearly, for the total duration, or, simply unknown to the borrower. The unknown category invariably indicates the borrower's ignorance about the basis of interest calculations, though as we shall see shortly, this category apparently includes a large category of loans at zero interest rates. Anyway, the 2nd row from bottom of this table indicates the distribution of loans across various categories, in which annual basis forms the most dominant category (39.35 %), followed by total loan duration, monthly basis, and daily basis and 'couldn't say' with weights of 29.55 %, 27.31 %, 2.06 % and 1.72 %, respectively. Large variations in these weights across loan sources seem to suggest the stylized patterns of these sources, as per borrower information. The dominant basis of interest rate calculation is annual for both formal-1 and formal-2 sources (96.97 % and 95.00 %, respectively), although the borrowers from these two sources have also cited monthly and total loan duration as basis for interest rate calculation, as per their understanding. Monthly rates constitute the dominant pattern in both segments of the semi-formal sector (with shares of 93.65 % and 100 %, respectively). In informal-1, there is a tilt towards monthly and

Table 4.2A: Loan Cases Classified on the Basis of Interest Rate Calculations and Sources

Loan Source	*Basis of Interest Rate*					
Frequency *Percent* *Row Percent*	*Couldn't Say*	*Daily*	*Monthly*	*Annual*	*Total Loan Duration*	*Total*
Informal-2	9 1.55 4.17	3 0.52 1.39	44 7.56 20.37	3 0.52 1.39	157 26.98 72.69	216 37.11
Informal-1	1 0.17 2.00	0 0.00 0.00	34 5.84 68.00	3 0.52 6.00	12 2.06 24.00	50 8.59
Semi-formal-2	0 0.00 0.00	0 0.00 0.00	20 3.44 100.00	0 0.00 0.00	0 0.00 0.00	20 3.44
Semi-formal-1	0 0.00 0.00	1 0.17 1.59	59 10.14 93.65	1 0.17 1.59	2 0.34 3.17	63 10.82
Formal-2	0 0.00 0.00	8 1.37 4.00	1 0.17 0.50	190 32.65 95.00	1 0.17 0.50	200 34.36
Formal-1	0 0.00 0.00	0 0.00 0.00	1 0.17 3.03	32 5.50 96.97	0 0.00 0.00	33 5.67
Total	10 1.72	12 2.06	159 27.32	229 39.35	172 29.55	582 100.00

daily rates (with shares of loan cases as 68.00 % and 20.37 %, respectively), though there are quite a few cases of annual and total loan period as basis of interest rate calculation. In informal-2, the inclination is more (compared to all loan cases) towards total duration (72.69 %), and monthly rate (20.37 %) as basis of interest rate calculation. In other words, compared to the formal and semi-formal sources, informal sources do have the capability to make loans where the basis of interest rate calculation is daily, total loan duration, or even ambiguous, which the other sources can't easily replicate.

Table 4.2B: Modes of Interest Rate Collection across Loan Sources

Loan Source	*Interest Charged*			
Frequency *Percent* *Row Percent*	*Zero*	*Flat*	*Diminishing Balance*	*Total*
Informal-2	16 2.75 7.41	182 31.27 84.26	18 3.09 8.33	216 37.11
Informal-1	0 0.00 0.00	45 7.73 90.00	5 0.86 10.00	50 8.59
Semi-formal-2	0 0.00 0.00	17 2.92 85.00	3 0.52 15.00	20 3.44
Semi-formal-1	0 0.00 0.00	14 2.41 22.22	49 8.42 77.78	63 10.82
Formal-2	8 1.37 4.00	10 1.72 5.00	182 31.27 91.00	200 34.36
Formal-1	0 0.00 0.00	1 0.17 3.03	32 5.50 96.97	33 5.67
Total	24 4.12	269 46.22	289 49.66	582 100.00

Modes of interest rate collection are analyzed in Table 4.2B. Among the 582 loan cases, as many as 40 % have zero interest rate, 46.22 % have interest charged on flat basis, and 49.66 % cases have interest charged on diminishing balance. In the two formal sources, interest charged on diminishing balance is the dominant pattern (96.97 % and 91.00 %, respectively), though for both formal-1 and formal-2, some cases of flat interest charges (18.60 % and 5.00 %, respectively) are also observed. In semi-formal-1, diminishing balance is the dominant pattern (77.48 %

cases), whereas in semi-formal-2, interest charged on flat rate basis is the dominant pattern (85.00 % cases). In informal-1, there is more than average inclination towards use of both flat rate and diminishing balance formulae, though the incidence of the former is found to be much more (90.00 %) than that of the latter (only 10.00 %). In informal-2, the dominant pattern is flat interest (84.26 %), though there are quite a few cases of interest charging on zero and diminishing balance mode (7.41 % and 8.33 %, respectively). Thus, while both formal sources and semi-formal-1 have an overwhelming tendency to charge interest on diminishing balance format, this is definitely not true of semi-formal-2 and informal-1 sources, and especially of the former. Informal-2, on the other hand, makes use of all three modalities, though in overwhelming proportion of cases they charge merely zero interest rate—apparently in the spirit of helping good neighbors in times need!

Table 4.2C: Incidence of Upfront Collection of Interest and Extent of Incentives (through lower interest rate) for Repayment on Time/Earlier

Loan Source	*Upfront Collection of Interest and Extent of Incentives*		
Frequency *Percent* *Row Percent*	*Incidence of Upfront Collection of Interest*	*Extent of Incentives for Loan Repayment on/Before Time*	*Total*
Informal-2	214 36.77 99.07	2 0.34 0.93	216 37.11
Informal-1	48 8.25 96.00	2 0.34 4.00	50 8.59
Semi-formal-2	7 1.20 35.00	13 2.23 65.00	20 3.44
Semi-formal-1	61 10.48 96.83	2 0.34 3.17	63 10.82
Formal-2	199 34.19 99.50	1 0.17 0.50	200 34.36
Formal-1	33 5.67 100.00	0 0.00 0.00	33 5.67
Total	562 96.56	20 3.44	582 100.00

Table 4.2C describes incidence of upfront collection of interest as well as the extent of incentives used by lending agencies for loan repayment on/before time. Incidence of upfront collection of interest is found to be highest among formal-1 lenders (9%) followed by formal 2 and semi-informal 1. On the other hand, if we look at the extent of use of incentives to induce loan repayment on/before time, semi-formal-2 source has the highest record of 65%, followed by informal-1 (4%) and semi-formal-1 (3.17%). This devise is used in only 0.93% cases by informal-2 and in 0.5% cases by formal-2, while formal-1 doesn't at all use this devise. Obviously, in respect of providing incentives for timely loan repayment, the semi-formal-2 seems to be quite ahead of others.

4.4 ANALYSIS OF LOAN PURPOSES

In course of this study, the borrowers were asked to reveal the main purpose for which loans were taken from different sources, though they may not be always using the loan for the stated purpose.[1] Loans are found to be taken for three main purposes—as input in production (51.20% of cases), to support consumption (44.16%), and also for human capital investment (for example, for education, medical treatment and marriages), the incidence of the last category being only 4.64%. It can be seen from the rows of Table 4.3 that both formal and semi-formal-2 sectors have more than average tilt towards providing production loans, with their shares being 84.85%, 81% and 85%, respectively. The share of semi-formal-1 source in production loan is 63.49% i.e., slightly more than the average incidence of production loans (51.20%). Formal-1 and formal-2 sources provide very little in the form of consumption loan, their reported figures being only 9.09% and 17.50%, respectively, and these two figures too must be reflecting adverse usage of production loans. The two semi-formal sectors does not provide any significant amounts of consumption loans (19.05% and 15.0%, respectively). Large chunks of consumption loan come from informal-1 and informal-2 sources, and especially the latter (with an overwhelming share of 82.41%). Semi-formal-1 source has the strongest orientation towards supporting human capital investment (17.46%), while the shares of informal-1 and formal-1 are 18% and 6%, respectively (but these two figures are still higher than the average figure of 4.64% of human capital loans). Thus, it is seen that informal-2 is the major source of supply of consumption loans, though informal-1 and the two semi-formal sources also support consumption loans. As consumption

[1]This means, incidence of adverse usage of loans is not ruled out.

loans are not generally supported by the formal sources of credit, it is only through adverse usage of production loans that consumption gets some support from the formal credit sources. The semi-formal sources seem to have been supporting all three types of loans, though their major thrust is towards production loans, for understandable reasons. The flexibility as shown by semi-formal and informal sources towards openly supporting consumption loan is a point which is often lost sight of in providing adequate space to these sectors in our policy exercises.

Table 4.3: Loan Cases Classified by Reported Purpose and Sources

Loan Source	*Purpose of Loan*			
Frequency Percent Row Percent	*Reported Purpose: Production*	*Reported Purpose: Human Capital Investment*	*Reported Purpose: Consumption*	*Total Loan Cases*
Informal-2	31 5.33 14.35	7 1.20 3.24	178 30.58 82.41	216 37.11
Informal-1	20 3.44 40.00	4 0.69 8.00	26 4.47 52.00	50 8.59
Semi-formal-2	17 2.92 85.00	0 0.00 0.00	3 0.52 15.00	20 3.44
Semi-formal-1	40 6.87 63.49	11 1.89 17.46	12 2.06 19.05	63 10.82
Formal-2	162 27.84 81.00	3 0.52 1.50	35 6.01 17.50	200 34.36
Formal-1	28 4.81 84.85	2 0.34 6.06	3 0.52 9.09	33 5.67
Total	298 51.20	27 4.64	257 44.16	582 100.00

4.5 USES OF LOAN COLLATERALS

Being an inter-temporal transaction between two parties, credit almost invariably demands a token of trust from the borrower to the lender. This token of trust is referred to as security or collateral, which the borrower has to produce to get a loan. Whereas the formal credit sources have traditionally insisted on marketable collaterals, the informal sources are always found to create loans even against non-marketable or no collateral.

This section attempts to describe the types of collaterals being used by the rural lenders in the present context, and to ascertain whether or not there is a systematic pattern in the use of collaterals by the various loan sources.

Table 4.4A describes the various types of collaterals used in the present context. Among the 582 loan cases arising among the sample borrowers, in as much as 37.29% cases, there is no security or collateral. Almost 85% of the loans produced by informal-2 sources belong to this category, as these types of lenders, because of their proximity to and intimate knowledge of the borrowers, are in a position to provide loans without collateral. Semi-formal-2 also produce some amount of loans without collateral (10%). The second most important type of collateral used is mortgage of farmland (27%). The two formal sources and informal-1 have a strong liking for this type of collateral, weightage of this collateral in their loan portfolio being 90.91%, 58.50% and 20.00%, respectively. The third most important type of collateral used is group guarantee, thanks to the SHG movement taking place in this part of the globe. It has an overall weightage of 13.40%. The two semi-formal sources have a strong liking for this type of collateral. Importance of group guarantee in their loan portfolios of these lenders is 93.65% and 90%, respectively. Although except semi-formally all loan sources seem to have entertained this collateral, only informal-1 seems to have a strong inclination towards use of this collateral, the importance of this collateral to them being 32.00%, respectively. Agreement for interlinking (input purchase, pledge for output sale) is relatively less frequently used form of collateral with weight of 15.98%. Only cooperatives (i.e., formal 2 source) are in a position to use interlinked input sale and output sale transaction as collaterals against credit. Both formal-1 and informal-2 sources have displayed their interest in using interlinking as collateral against loan. Thus, we observe an important pattern in the use of collateral by different sources. Although all sources provide some loans against no security, it is only informal-2 source, which seems to have strong advantage in producing loans against no security or collateral. Third party guarantee is used to some extent as collateral by formal-1 and formal-2 but informal-1 has a strong inclination towards use of this collateral. Group guarantee is never or hardly used as collateral by the two informal sources. But this is the predominant form of collateral to the two semi-formal sources, whereas, thanks to the SHG movement, the two formal sources are also making use of this collateral. For structural reasons, formal-1 source usually demands either farmland or residential property or a non-residential asset as collateral. Informal-1 source also make use of these three assets as collateral, but importance of these assets as collateral seem to have come down considerably from what these assets used to be in more traditional settings. Of these three types of physical assets, cooperatives use only farmland as collateral.

Table 4.4A: Loan Cases Classified by Collaterals Used and Sources

Loan Sources	*Security or Collateral*					
Frequency Percent Row Percent	*No Security*	*Interlinking*	*Third Party*	*Group Guarantee*	*Mortgage*	*Total*
Informal-2	184 31.62 85.19	15 2.58 6.94	16 2.75 7.41	1 0.17 0.46	0 0.00 0.00	216 37.11
Informal-1	24 4.12 48.00	0 0.00 0.00	16 2.75 32.00	0 0.00 0.00	10 1.72 20.00	50 8.59
Semi-formal-2	2 0.34 10.00	0 0.00 0.00	0 0.00 0.00	18 3.09 90.00	0 0.00 0.00	20 3.44
Semi-formal-1	4 0.69 6.35	0 0.00 0.00	0 0.00 0.00	59 10.14 93.65	0 0.00 0.00	63 10.82
Formal-2	2 0.34 1.00	77 13.23 38.50	4 0.69 2.00	0 0.00 0.00	117 20.10 58.50	200 34.36
Formal-1	1 0.17 3.03	1 0.17 3.03	1 0.17 3.03	0 0.00 0.00	30 5.15 90.91	33 5.67
Total	217 37.29	93 15.98	37 6.36	78 13.40	157 26.98	582 100.00

Thanks to the SHG movement throughout the world, thrift habit among poor borrowers is being encouraged so much so that saving deposits of SHGs with banks can act as collateral for their future loans. The importance of borrower's deposit with lenders is shown in Table 4.4B. It is seen that the incidence of deposits with lender is only 1% for the two informal sources. However, formal and semi-informal sources are making immense use of borrower's deposits with them in building up their confidence to extend loans to such borrowers. The semi-formal-2 source, i.e., NBFCs, theoretically speaking cannot take deposits from borrowers, but almost always they do take a small amount of security deposit while making loans. The two formal sources seem to have taken deposits from borrowers in 78% and 60% cases, respectively, whereas the two semi-formal sources have done it in 81% and 77% cases, respectively. Thus, placing some deposits with the lender acts as a good act of trust on the part of the borrower to induce the lender to make loans. The two informal sources, because of their proximity and intimacy, probably don't need this devise, but this a healthy devise for making loans in the context of both formal and semi-formal lenders.

Table 4.4B: Incidence (proportion) of Loan Cases having Deposits with Lender Classified by Loan Source

Loan Sources	*Proportion of Loan Cases with Borrower Having Deposit with Lender*
Formal-2	0.60
Formal-1	0.78
Semi-formal-2	0.77
Semi-formal-1	0.81
Informal-2	0.01
Informal-1	0.01

4.6 TERMS AND CONDITIONS FOR LOAN REPAYMENTS

Tables 4.5A provide for maximum number of installments in loan re-payments (27.57). This is expected because most of them insist on weekly or fortnightly repayments to suit the cash flow patterns of their borrowers. As we have seen earlier in Table 4.1, both the formal sources provide loans for a fairly large duration (for approximately 20 and 11 months, respectively). Formal-1 sector is found to provide for 13.44 numbers of installments, whereas formal-2 has provided for about 8 installments on average. As compared to semi-formal-2, semi-formal-1 provides loans for shorter duration (about 9 months as compared to 13 for the former) as

Table 4.5A: Terms and Conditions of Loan Repayment Classified by Sources

Loan Sources	*Repayment Installments*	*Proportion of Cases with Lump Sum Repayment*	*Proportion of Cases with Holiday Period Allowed in Repayment*
Informal-2	2.36	0.84	0.05
Informal-1	6.17	0.53	0.01
Semi-formal-2	27.57	0.09	0.09
Semi-formal-1	8.97	0.27	0.04
Formal-2	7.87	0.73	0.13
Formal-1	13.44	0.16	0.05

well as smaller number of installments (about 9 as compared to 27). Although both informal sources are providing moderately long-duration loans (about 10 and 11 months, respectively), they seem to be in favor of lesser number of repayment installments (6 and 2 respectively). This is especially true of the informal-2 source.

Table 4.5B: Flexibility Rankings in Terms Loan Repayment of Loan Cases by Sources

Loan Sources	*Rankings in Terms of Flexibility in a Descending Order with 1 as Highest Flexibility*					
	1	*2*	*3*	*4*	*5*	*All loans*
Formal-2	67 (34.72)	67 (34.72)	48 (24.87)	11 (5.70)	0 (0.00)	193 (100.00)
Formal-1	4 (9.30)	8 (18.60)	27 (62.79)	4 (9.40)	0 (0.00)	43 (100.00)
Semi-formal-2	5 (22.73)	3 (13.64)	7 (31.64)	4 (18.18)	3 (13.64)	22 (100.00)
Semi-formal-1	3 (5.66)	6 (11.32)	23 (43.40)	17 (32.08)	4 (7.55)	53 (100.00)
Informal-2	44 (21.05)	83 (39.71)	59 (28.23)	18 (8.61)	5 (2.39)	209 (100.00)
Informal-1	16 (29.63)	15 (27.78)	10 (18.52)	10 (18.52)	3 (5.56)	54 (100.00)
Total	139 (24.22)	182 (31.71)	174 (30.31)	64 (11.15)	15 (2.61)	574 (100.00)

Note: Figures in parentheses represent row percentages.

Column 3 of Table 4.5A highlights the incidence of lump sum repayment of loans. The highest incidence of lump sum repayment is observed in informal-2 source (84%), followed by formal-2, i.e., cooperatives (73%), traditional rural moneylenders, i.e., informal-1 (53%). The provision for lump sum repayments is relatively less in semi-formal-1, formal-1 and semi-formal-2 (27%, 16%, and 9%, respectively).

Incidence of holiday period allowed in repayment of loans is rather small, (column 4 of Table 4.5A). However, on this count, the cooperatives are found to have provided maximum flexibility (13%) followed by semi-formal-2 (9%), formal-1 and informal-2 (5% each), and semi-formal-1 (4%). Provision for such holidays is found to be least (only 1%) for loans from informal-1 source. In terms of overall flexibility in loan repayment in the judgment of the borrowers (shown in Table 4.5B), certain sources seem to have displayed more flexibility as compared to others. If we look at the row percentages of this table, it becomes clear that both formal sources and semi-formal-2, have displayed much more flexibility as compared to the commercial banking sector and the two semi-formal sources. While commercial banks and RRBs (i.e., formal-1) seem to be somewhere in the middle in terms of flexibility ranking, both semi-formal sources seem to have a tilt towards the relatively rigid range. The ranking distribution for traditional moneylenders looks more uniformly spread as compared to those of others, though their distributions seem to have humps towards both ends (i.e., the distribution becomes u-shaped), thereby indicating that this source tends to take both relatively flexible and relatively rigid approach with respect to different subsets of borrowers. This is expected, given the locational advantages and local monopoly power of these lenders, which allow them to apply discriminatory devises more easily as compared to the other loan sources.

4.7 INCIDENCE OF LOAN OVERDUE AND THE REASONS THEREOF

Table 4.6A and Table 4.6B describe the situation. In the former, percentage of overdue is reported in columns 2 and 3 in terms of numbers and amount of loan defaulted, respectively. Contrary to common belief, default rate is moderately high for the two informal sources (12.31% and 18.46%, respectively), in terms of loans cases, and 5.40% and 5.98%, respectively, in terms of loan amount. Both formal sources are generally entrusted responsibility of making large number of small loans to their borrowers in the presence of various government schemes. As a result, it is no surprise that percentage of loan amount overdue in formal sectors is generally smaller (9.51% and 5.02%, respectively), as compared to percentage of loan overdue cases (25.38% and 16.15%, respectively). However, both types of figures are relatively high for these two sectors as compared to others, for understandable reasons. SHG groups promoted by government/NABARD/NGOs, i.e., semi-formal-1 source has only 4.62% of loan overdue cases and 2.38% of loan amount overdue, thus displaying best performance against defaults, as compared to other credit sources. In contrast, NBFC-promoted MFIs, i.e., semi-formal-2 source have 8.08% and 4.50% overdue in terms of loan cases and loan amounts, respectively.

Table 4.6B highlights the reasons for loan default as cited by the borrowers. In about 52% cases the borrowers could not tell exactly the reason for default. Whenever they could cite reasons, prominent among them are crop failure (roughly 11%), capacity failure or daughter's marriage (roughly 23%), low profit or poor income (roughly 5%), and adverse climatic condition (roughly 11%). The phenomenon of loan

Table 4.6A: Incidence of Loan Overdue across Loan Sources

Loan Sources	*% of Cases of Loan Overdue*	*% of Loan Amount Overdue*
Formal-1(4333)	25.38	9.54
Formal-2 (200)	16.15	5.02
Semi-formal-1 (63)	4.62	2.38
Semi-formal-2 (20)	8.08	4.50
Informal-1 (50)	12.31	5.40
Informal-2 (216)	18.46	5.98

Note: Figures in parentheses represent numbers of loan cases arising out of the sample households.

Table 4.6B: Loan Overdue (i.e., default) Cases Classified by Cited Reasons and Source

Loan Sources	*Reasons of Overdue*					
Frequency Percent Row Percent	*Couldn't Say*	*Crop Failure*	*Adverse Climatic Condition*	*Capacity Failure/ Daughter's Marriage*	*Low Profit/ Poor Income*	*Total Number of Default Cases*
Informal-2	7 10.77 58.33	1 1.54 8.33	0 0.00 0.00	4 6.15 33.33	0 0.00 0.00	12 18.46
Informal-1	3 4.62 37.50	0 0.00 0.00	3 4.62 37.50	1 1.54 12.50	1 1.54 12.50	8 12.31
Semi-formal-2	2 3.08 100.00	0 0.00 0.00	0 0.00 0.00	0 0.00 0.00	0 0.00 0.00	2 3.08
Semi-formal-1	2 3.08 66.67	0 0.00 0.00	0 0.00 0.00	0 0.00 0.00	1 1.54 33.33	3 4.62
Formal-2	13 20.00 43.33	5 7.69 16.67	4 6.15 13.33	8 12.31 26.67	0 0.00 0.00	30 46.15
Formal-1	7 10.77 70.00	1 1.54 10.00	0 0.00 0.00	2 3.08 20.00	0 0.00 0.00	10 15.38
Total	34 52.31	7 10.77	7 10.77	15 23.08	2 3.08	65 100.00

Note: Figures in parentheses represent row percentages.

overdue seems most glaring among the formal sources of credit. It is important to point out that capacity failure/daughter's marriage and crop failure are the most predominant reasons for loan default with respect to two formal sources. In formal-2, adverse climatic condition is another reason for default (13.33 %). In informal-1, reasons for loan default are fairly distributed across the last 3 cited reasons, though default is relatively prominent for reason of adverse climatic condition. In informal-2, on the other hand, the capacity failure/daughter's marriage is most predominant reason (33 %) for default.

4.8 RECOURSES GENERALLY AVAILABLE TO BORROWERS IN CASES OF NON-WILLFUL DEFAULT

Cases of loan default arise not merely because of borrower opportunism (i.e., willful default), but also because of unforeseen contingencies beyond control of borrowers, which are generally referred to as 'locking-in effect' or non-willful default. In all loan cases, which arose out of the sample borrowers, the borrowers were asked hypothetical question about what recourse they would resort to in case of non-willful default. The major recourses, as cited by the borrowers are classified in Table 4.7. From this table, it is found that the most prominent recourse cited is request for postponement of interest repayment (about 65 %), followed by request for extra credit dose (about 18 %), requesting for allowing liquidation of asset (about 12 %). In case of formal-2 loans, the prominent recourses are postponement of interest payment, asking for extra dose of credit and allowing liquidation of asset, in descending order of importance. For loans from semi-formal-2, the dominant reasons are postponement of interest repayment followed by request extra credit dose postponement of loan repayment. Both these sources entertain to some extent request for allowing credit. For traditional moneylenders the prominent recourses are postponement of interest repayment, request for extra credit dose and allowing liquidation of asset in declining order of importance. This source too entertains some small percentage of postponement of loan repayment. Table 4.7, therefore, gives an idea of how much flexibility or shock absorption capacity is displayed to the borrowers by different sources of credit. There is no doubt that formal-2 and informal-2 display the maximum order of flexibility or shock absorption power to help the borrowers in the face of unforeseen contingencies. The semi-formal-1 and even informal-1 source display considerable flexibility, unlike the formal-1 and semi-formal-2. It is therefore no surprise that in spite of rapid expansion of the network of commercial banks and RRBs, they have not been able to achieve an inclusive system of loan disbursal, as compared to the two semi-formal and two informal sources. If we are interested in a healthy system of credit delivery for the rural masses, probably we need to appreciate the strengths of the other loan sources, in spite of their weaknesses, while at the same time highlighting the need for learning important lessons for formal-1 source from others.

Table 4.7: Loan Cases Classified by Source and Recourses Available to Borrowers in Cases of Non-Willful Default

Loan Source	*Recourses*					
Frequency Percent Row Percent	*Request Postponement of Loan Repayment*	*Request Postponement of Interest Repayment*	*Request Extra Credit Dose*	*Allow Liquidation of Asset*	*Couldn't Respond Anything*	*Total*
Informal-2	5 0.86 2.31	180 30.93 83.33	14 2.41 6.48	15 2.58 6.94	2 0.34 0.93	216 37.11
Informal-1	1 0.17 2.00	25 4.30 50.00	17 2.92 34.00	3 0.52 6.00	4 0.69 8.00	50 8.59
Semi-formal-2	2 0.34 10.00	12 2.06 60.00	5 0.86 25.00	1 0.17 5.00	0 0.00 0.00	20 3.44
Semi-formal-1	0 0.00 0.00	47 8.08 74.60	10 1.72 15.87	4 0.69 6.35	2 0.34 3.17	63 10.82
Formal-2	0 0.00 0.00	101 17.35 50.50	52 8.93 26.00	41 7.04 20.50	6 1.03 3.00	200 34.36
Formal-1	0 0.00 0.00	17 2.92 51.52	7 1.20 21.21	4 0.69 12.12	5 0.86 15.15	33 5.67
Total	8 1.37	382 65.64	105 18.04	68 11.68	19 3.26	582 100.00

4.9 SUMMARY AND CONCLUSION

Credit being a package of services provided and repaid over a period of time has multifarious attributes beyond merely its quantity and price—namely, the interest rate. In this chapter, therefore an attempt is made rural to understand variations in the multifarious attributes of credit, besides bringing out the stylized patterns therein. The stylized observations together with policy implications are as follows:

- The statistical significance of the various loan sources becomes clear from the fact that 37.11% loan cases arose from informal-2 source, followed by 34.32% share of formal-2, i.e., the cooperative sector. The informal moneylenders (informal-1) and SHGs formed by government/NABARD/NGOs (i.e., semi-formal-1) have shares of 8.50% and 10.82%, respectively. The formal commercial banking sectors and

RRBs, capture only 5.67% share, whereas NBFC-promoted MFIs has a meager share of 3.43%. In spite of deliberate choice of pockets where MFIs have been functioning, they (i.e., semi-formal-1 and semi-formal-2) could not cover more than 14% loan cases.

- Among the various loan sources, both informal sources and the cooperative sector have the longest years of association with the rural borrowers. The vast experiences of these sources needs to be carefully made use of cannot framing any useful policy towards rural credit.
- For large loans, there is hardly any substitute for formal-1 source, which is also to the liking of this source for transaction cost reasons. Cooperatives, on the other hand seem to have developed a niche for supplying medium-sized loans. Among the other sources, there seems to be much more competition in supply of small to medium-sized loans. Probably policy makers need to fine-tune policy around this natural division of labor among loan sources in catering to different sizes of loans.
- It is also observed that only some sources, cooperatives in particular, because of the nature of their operations and locational advantages, have comparative advantages in supplying a part of the loan in kind, taking advantage of complementarities between credit and a few pertinent services the borrower needs for effective use of credit. Thus, cooperatives are natural choice for implementing credit-plus policy.
- In terms of average duration of loans, the comparable strengths of NBFCs, cooperatives and the two forms of informal lenders deserve special attention for purpose of policy.
- Although, interest rates can't be compared unless and until the loan cycle, as well as the borrower's production or consumption cycle are also taken into consideration, in terms of annual average figures, interest rates of both formal sources, semi-formal-1 and even informal-2 sources are somewhat comparable. This rate is least for cooperatives, and second-least for commercial banks and RRBs. The estimated annual figure is the highest for traditional moneylenders (55%), as expected. So, policy must attempt to generate alternatives to replace moneylenders, which can offer similar services at lower rates to the borrowers.
- Regarding basis of interest rate calculation, it is mostly annual for both formal-1 and formal-2 sources (96.9% and 95.00%, respectively). Monthly rates constitute the dominant pattern in both segments of the semi-formal sector (with shares of 93.65% and 100.00%, respectively). In informal-1, there is a tilt towards monthly and daily rates (with shares of loan cases as 68.00% and 20.37%, respectively),

In informal-2, the inclination is more (compared to all loan cases) towards borrower total duration (72.69 %), and monthly rate (20.37 %) as basis of interest rate calculation. Thus, compared to the formal and semi-formal sources, informal sources do have the capability to make loans where the basis of interest rate calculation is monthly, total loan duration, or even ambiguous, which the other sources don't find it easy to replicate.

- On modes of interest rate collection, both formal sources and semi-formal-1 have an overwhelming tendency to charge interest on diminishing balance format, while this is definitely not true of semi-formal-2 and informal-1 sources, and especially of the former. Informal-2, on the other hand, makes use of all three modalities, though in overwhelming proportion of cases they charge merely zero interest rate—apparently in the spirit of helping good neighbors in times need! So, finally an alternative source to replicate this virtue of informal-2 source looks like a nearly impossible task.
- In respect of providing incentives for timely loan repayment, the two formal sources find it imperative for them to be quite pro-active as compared to other sources. As the extent of loan default is relatively less, the semi-formal sources probably don't have a strong urge to use this devise.
- Loans are found to be taken for three main purposes—as input for production (51.20 % of cases), to support consumption (44.16 %), and also for human capital investment (for example, for education, medical treatment and marriages), the incidence of the last category being only 4.64 %. Informal-2 source seems to be the major source of supply of consumption loans, though informal-1 and the two semi-formal sources also support consumption loans as a matter of policy. As consumption loans are not generally supported by the formal sources of credit, it is only through adverse usage of production loans that consumption gets some support from the formal credit sources. The flexibility as shown by semi-formal and informal sources towards openly supporting consumption loan is a point which is often lost sight of in providing adequate space to these sectors in our policy exercises.
- It is found that there is indeed a systematic pattern in the use of collaterals by the various loan sources. Although all sources provide some loans against no security, it is only informal-2 source, which seems to have strong advantage in producing loans against no security or collateral. Personal guarantee is used to some extent as collateral by almost all sources, but only informal-1 and semi-formal-2 have a

strong inclination towards use of this collateral. Group guarantee is never or hardly used as collateral by the two informal sources. But this is the predominant form of collateral to the two semi-formal sources, whereas, thanks to the SHG movement, the two formal sources are also making use of this collateral. For structural reasons, formal-1 source usually demands either farm land or residential property or a non-residential asset as collateral. Of the three types of physical assets, cooperatives use only farm land as collateral.

- Formal loan sources merely take deposits from borrowers (in 78 % and 60 % cases, respectively), whereas the two semi-formal sources have done it in 81 % and 77 % cases, respectively (the latter taking it in the form of security deposit). The two informal sources, because of their proximity and intimacy, don't use this devise.
- Regarding loan repayment format, semi-formal-2 source, insists on weekly or fortnightly repayments to suit the cash flow patterns of their borrowers. As both the formal sources provide loans for a fairly large duration (for approximately 19 and 11 months, respectively), they are found to provide on average 13.44 and 8 installments, respectively. As compared to semi-formal-2, semi-formal-1 provides loans for shorter duration (about 9 months as compared to 14 for the former) as well as smaller number of installments (about 9 as compared to 28). Although both informal sources are providing moderately long-duration loans (about 11 and 12 months, respectively), they seem to be in favor of lesser number of repayment installments (6 and 2, respectively).
- On possibility of lump sum repayment of loans, the highest incidence is observed in informal-2 source (84 %), followed by formal-2 (73 %) and informal-1 (53 %). The provision for lump sum repayments is relatively less in semi-formal-1, formal-1 and semi-formal-2 (27 %, 16 %, and 9 %, respectively).
- In terms of overall flexibility in loan repayment certain sources like cooperatives and two types of informal lenders seem to have displayed more flexibility as compared to the commercial banking sector and the two semi-formal sources. While commercial banks and RRBs (i.e., formal-1) seem to be somewhere in the middle in terms of flexibility ranking, both semi-formal sources seem to have a tilt towards the relatively rigid range.
- As both formal sources are generally entrusted responsibility of making large number of small loans under various government schemes, it is no surprise that percentage of loan amount overdue in formal sectors is generally smaller (9.54 % and 5.02 %, respectively), as

compared to percentage of loan overdue cases (25.38% and 16.51%, respectively). However, both types of figures are relatively high for these two sectors as compared to other sources. SHG groups promoted by government/NABARD/NGOs has only 4.62% of loan overdue cases and 2.38% of loan amount overdue, thus displaying the best performance against defaults. In contrast, NBFC-promoted MFIs, i.e., semi-formal-2 source have 8.08% and 4.50% overdue in terms of loan cases and loan amounts, respectively.

- Prominent among the cited reasons against loan default are capacity failure or daughter's marriage (23.08%), crop failure (10.77%) and adverse climatic condition (10%). The phenomenon of loan overdue seems most glaring among the formal sources of credit with crop failure as the most predominant reason for default. In informal-1 and informal-2, reasons for loan default are fairly distributed across the four cited reasons. Loan default is negligible for two semi-formal sources.
- The major recourses, as cited by the borrowers against non-willful default are: request for postponement of interest repayment (65.64%), followed by request for extra credit (18%), allowing liquidation of asset (another 11%). While formal-2 and informal-2 display the maximum flexibility or shock absorption power to help the borrowers in the face of unforeseen contingencies, the semi-formal-1 sources and even informal-1 source display considerable flexibility, unlike the semi-formal-2, commercial banking sector and RRBs. So, for a healthy system of credit delivery for the rural masses, probably we need to appreciate the strengths of the other loan sources, in spite of their certain demonstrated weaknesses, while at the same time highlighting the need for formal-1 source to learn important lessons from others.

A detailed probe into the terms and conditions of credit across sectors has revealed that credit has multifarious attributes beyond price and quantity, and that no source seems to have point-wise dominance over others. In fact, there is a high degree of complementarity across sources. Given the fact that all informal/semi-formal sources have solid reasons for their co existence, it is no more than wishful thinking on the part of some policy makers to get rid of informal and semi-formal sources. In this situation, our policy should rather recognize this complementarity and tap it to the fullest possible extent to the benefit of different segments of rural borrowers. The commercial banking sectors, including RRBs, seem to have comparative advantages in producing larger size loans with little credit plus services. Cooperatives, given their vast network and long standing experience, seem to have comparative advantages in producing small to medium size loans. Provided cooperatives are free from their vices and weaknesses through sufficient cooperative sector reforms, they along with government/NABARD/NGO-promoted SHGs may be entrusted the task of managing various government schemes at minimum transaction cost from both the sides. The fact that NBFC-promoted MFIs have come into existence to play an important role filling in the gaps and deficiencies in formal and informal credit, ought to be looked upon as a matter of relief, rather than with a vengeance. As these sources can't be wished away, it is better to evolve careful processes and policies to make them more transparent, competitive and accountable from the viewpoints of borrowers. When credit plus credit-complementary services must go as a package to small borrowers, there is ample reason to support simultaneous blooming of all non-commercial bank/RRB sources.

CHAPTER 5

Estimating Borrower Transaction Costs

5.1 INTRODUCTION

In the absence of any suitable data available from lending organizations, in this chapter we shall limit ourselves to an attempt to estimate borrower transaction cost across various credit sources. In a perfectly competitive world with full information available at zero cost, homogenous products and instantaneous transactions (i.e., purchase and sale taking place at the same point in time), there is no transaction cost. This means there is no cost involved of the two parties in a transaction beyond what is paid for sale and purchase of a product/service—this means, the seller receives exactly what the buyer pays in exchange for the product/service in question. In other words, neither the seller nor the borrower incurs any additional expenditure while making the transaction. In a real world, however things are not so simple broadly because of three reasons: (i) bounded rationality—i.e., human behavior is intentionally rational but limitedly so because of informational lacuna, so that cost is incurred in gathering and processing information, (ii) opportunism or moral hazard, i.e., the parties to a transaction may engage in cheating each other, which means their promises are not necessarily fulfilled in practice, and they need to put special efforts for monitoring and enforcement, and (iii) locking-in effect arising because of unforeseen contingencies, which are beyond the control of the two sides of a transaction. In the context of a credit transaction, these problems arise in boundless manner because credit invariably involves transfer of resources between two sides over a period of time, within which so many things—whether intentional or unintentional—may occur. Moreover, credit being a service with multifarious attributes and conditionalities, invariably makes it prone to adverse selection of one party by the other (reflecting bounded rationality), willful default of loan or induced misappropriation of the collateral by the lender (both implying opportunism), and non-willful default due to unforeseen contingencies, which limits predicted behavior on the part of the borrower or the lender. It is therefore no surprise that both the sides to an act of credit—whether borrower or lender—must invest time, money and resources to minimize the problems of adverse selection, moral hazard and locking-in effect. Unfortunately, lender side information on transaction cost is not available from any of the lending institutions. So, we shall be focusing on borrower transaction cost alone in this chapter.

Some of the borrower transaction cost on search and taking precaution against unforeseen contingencies or against opportunistic behavior from the other side are unobservable and non-quantifiable in simple monetary terms. Only some of these costs are observable and can be expressed in monetary terms. Our intention in this chapter is to lay our fingers on only observable transaction costs, which can be expressed in monetary terms. Obviously, this attempt towards measurement or estimation of borrower transaction cost can be at best an imperfect one.

This chapter is organized as follows. The next section decomposes observed transaction cost of the borrower in terms of time/wage lost due to search of the right type of lender, and time cost incurred in waiting for the loan to get sanctioned and released on time. It also includes search cost in exploring potential lender for a loan, and expenses incurred on application, documentation and processing fees for getting a loan sanctioned. As a large number of costs are implicit, which cannot be captured through the market logic, our treatment of borrower transaction cost in this chapter is essentially a partial one. The last section summarizes the findings of this chapter.

5.2 SOME ESTIMATES OF BORROWER TRANSACTION COSTS

As mentioned earlier, our treatment of borrower transaction costs is far from a comprehensive one, as we are able to lay our fingers on only some of these explicit or implicit costs borne by the borrower, while only some of these can be expressed in monetary terms under appropriate assumptions. The types of borrower transaction costs discussed and estimated in this chapter are: costs incurred by the borrower in undertaking visits to the lender for getting loans (Table 5.1), borrower's search cost in exploring alternative lenders before approaching the final lender (Table 5.2), borrower's waiting cost in between application for and sanction of loan, and again between sanction of loan and its disbursement (Table 5.3), and borrower's explicit transaction cost in terms of application, documentation and processing fees (Table 5.4). These costs are added up, when these can be expressed in monetary terms. This is done in Table 5.5.

As it can be seen from Table 5.1, the borrower has paid the maximum number of visits to lender (3.39) for loans from commercial banking sources including RRBs. This cost is less but fairly similar for loans from NBFCs (2.40), and lesser for loans from cooperatives and government/NABARD/NGO-promoted SHGs (2.12 and 2.04, respectively). For traditional moneylenders, this figure is only 1.76, and lowest (0.84) for other informal rural money lending agencies. Travelling costs per visit and wage lost per visit, which reflects opportunity cost of time of borrowers from different sources, seem to have broadly a similar pattern—it is highest for loans from commercial banks cum RRBs, a bit less for NBFC loans, even less for loans from traditional moneylenders, cooperatives and government/NABARD/NGO-promoted SHGs, and the lowest for other informal rural money lending agencies. It is interesting to note that when we express this component of borrower transaction cost as percentage of the sanctioned loan amount, this figure turns out to be much higher for semi-formal lenders of both types and traditional moneylender (1.93%, 1.65% and 1.12%, respectively) as compared to loans from commercial banks cum RRBs and cooperatives (0.47% and 0.52%, respectively). This figure is once again the least (0.34%) for other informal rural lenders. The transaction cost advantage of the last group of informal rural

Table 5.1: Borrower Transaction Cost for Loans across Sources in Undertaking Visits to the Final Lender

(1)	*(2)*	*(3)*	*(4)*	*(5)*
Loan Sources	*# of Visits to Final Lender*	*Travelling Cost Per Visit*	*Wage Lost Per Visit*	*Transaction Cost on Visits to Final Lender as % of Loan Amount*
Informal-2 (216)	0.84 (216)	7.47 (216)	22.33 (214)	0.347
Informal-1 (50)	1.76 (50)	15.30 (50)	49.00 (50)	1.125
Semi-formal-2 (20)	2.40 (20)	21.75 (20)	71.25 (20)	1.932
Semi-formal-1 (63)	2.12 (63)	11.11 (63)	30.04 (63)	1.674
Formal-2 (200)	2.04 (200)	11.44 (200)	54.07 (200)	0.519
Formal-1 (33)	3.39 (33)	21.66 (33)	92.12 (33)	0.474

Note: Figures in parentheses represent # of loan cases for arriving at figures in each column. Variation in this number across the same row is due to missing entries on some variables, which the borrower failed to report.

lenders is well known. However, the lesser transaction cost of formal sector lenders as compared to semi-formal sector lenders can be attributed to the fact that the former provide much larger size loans on average (roughly ₹ 81,000 and 25,000, respectively) as compared to the same for the two semi-formal sector sources (roughly ₹ 5,200 and 11,500, respectively). In other words, while borrower transaction cost on this count may look large for formal sector loans and less for semi-formal sectors, this may be true in absolute terms but not true when expressed in relative percentage terms vis-à-vis the size of the loan.

In the rural context, the borrowers have found to have explored alternative sources before approaching their final lender. When, the borrower puts more effort in terms of number of alternatives explored and number of days lost therein, it may be looked upon as the importance he attaches to that particular kind of loan, on the one hand, and as the borrower's keenness to avoid the final source of credit, on the other. Columns 2, 3 and 4 in Table 5.2 displays number of alternatives explored, number of days lost in exploring and days lost per alternative explored (columns 2, 3 and 4, respectively). In first two columns, formal 1 source usually turned out to be the most costly, followed by semi-formal 1 and informal 2, whereas semi-formal 1 and informal 2 seem to appear on the lower end of the spectrum. If we evaluate borrower's travelling cost and wage cost in the same way, as we have done in columns 3 and 4 of Table 5.1, borrower's search cost as percentage of loan amount turned out be the highest (1.84%) for informal 1, followed by semi-formal 2, semi-formal 1, formal 1 and formal 2 (i.e., 1.69%, 1.47%, 0.47% and 0.41%, respectively). Once again, the search cost turns out to be the minimal (0.24%) for informal 2 lenders, thus explaining resilience of this lending group.

In terms of gap between application and approval of loan, on the one hand, and between sanction of a loan and its disbursement, on the other, formal 1 lenders have the least transaction cost advantages from borrower viewpoint, followed by formal 2, semi-formal 2, informal 1, semi-formal 1 and informal 2 lenders. Naturally, the same pattern holds across the different types of loan sources when one considers the overall gap between application and disbursement of loan (Table 5.3).

In terms of gap between application and approval of loan (column 2), and gap between sanction and disbursement of loan, informal 2 lender turns out to be the least, followed by informal 1, semi-formal 1 and semi-formal-2. Both these gaps are higher for formal lenders (12.97 and 13.52 respectively).

Table 5.2: Borrower Search Cost in Approaching Alternative Lenders before Visiting Final Lender Classified by Final Loan Source

(1)	*(2)*	*(3)*	*(4)*	*(5)*
Loan Sources	*# of Alternatives Explored*	*Days Lost in Exploring Alternatives*	*Days Lost Per Alternative Explored [(3)/(2)]*	*Borrower Search Cost in Exploring Alternatives to Final Lender as % of Loan Amount*
Informal-2 (216)	0.45 (216)	0.58 (214)	1.29	0.24
Informal-1 (50)	1.3 (50)	1.88 (50)	1.44	1.84
Semi-formal-2 (20)	2.1 (20)	2.1 (20)	1.00	1.69
Semi-formal-1 (63)	0.98 (63)	1.87 (62)	1.91	1.47
Formal-2 (200)	1.12 (200)	1.63 (200)	1.46	0.41
Formal-1 (33)	2.18 (33)	3.36 (33)	1.54	0.47

Note: Figures in parentheses represent # of loan cases for arriving at figures in each column. Variation in this number across the same row is due to missing entries on some variables, which the borrower failed to report.

Table 5.3: Borrower Transaction Cost in Terms of Waiting for Loan Sanctions and Loan Disbursement Classified by Loan Source

(1)	*(2)*	*(3)*	*(4)*
Loan Sources	*Gap between Application and Approval of Loan in Days*	*Gap between Sanction and Disbursement of Loan in Days*	*Gap between Application and Disbursement of Loan in Days [(2) + (3)]*
Informal-2 (216)	1.4 (216)	0.88 (216)	2.28
Informal-1(50)	2.98 (50)	1.52 (50)	4.5
Semi-formal-2 (20)	5.2 (20)	4.85 (20)	10.05
Semi-formal-1 (63)	4.51 (63)	4.24 (63)	8.75
Formal-2(200)	5.49 (200)	4.93 (200)	10.12
Formal-1 (33)	12.97 (33)	13.52 (33)	26.49

Note: Figures in parentheses represent # of loan cases for arriving at figures in each column. Variation in this number across the same row is due to missing entries on some variables, which the borrower failed to report.

Table 5.4 displays borrower expenditure on loan application, documentation and processing charges, besides showing the average pattern of whether or not loan documentation fee is exempted by the lender (0–1). In terms of application fee the two formal sources are the costliest, followed by the two semi-formal sectors in the intermediate range and the two informal sectors in the lowest range. In terms of documentation fee, formal 1 tops the list followed by semi-formal 2, formal 2, semi-formal 1, informal 2 and informal 1. Informal 2 provides the highest average order of flexibility in exempting the documentation fee, while formal 1 sector has absolutely no flexibility in this regard. Processing fee is the largest for semi-formal 2 and lowest (0) for informal 2 sector. In terms of overall transaction cost of this kind as percentage of loan amount, semi-formal 2 turns out to be the costliest, followed by formal 2, semi-formal 1, formal 1, informal 1 and informal 2. Here again, because the loan size is relatively large for formal sector sources, semi-formal loan turn out to be much costlier as compared to formal sector loans. Informal 2 sector is absolutely free of these costs.

Table 5.4: Borrower Transaction Cost in Terms of Application, Documentation and Processing Fees Classified by Loan Source

(1)	*(2)*	*(3)*	*(4)*	*(4)*	*(5)*
Loan Sources	*Expenditure on Loan Application in ₹*	*Expenditure on Documentation in ₹*	*Whether Exemption from Documentation Fee Allowed (0–1)*	*Processing Fee in ₹*	*Total Transaction Cost on Application, Documentation and Processing Fees in as % of Loan Amount*
Informal-2 (216)	0.1	0.19	0.98	0	0.00
Informal-1 (50)	0	1.2	0.88	0.2	0.01
Sem-formal-2 (20)	6.85	12.75	0.2	220	2.07
Semi-formal-1 (63)	0.87	1.9	0.89	1.59	0.08
Formal-2 (200)	17.9	7.85	0.15	0.1	0.10
Formal-1 (33)	29.33	15.15	0.03	15.45	0.07

Note: Figures in parentheses represent # of loan cases for arriving at figures in each column. Variation in this number across the same row is due to missing entries on some variables, which the borrower failed to report.

In Table 5.5, we put together the two types of monetized transaction cost of Tables 5.1–5.2, besides adding to it borrowers' transaction cost incurred on application fess documentation fees and processing fees. In terms of the first two types of transaction cost, the semi-formal 2 turns out to be the costliest source (3.62 %) followed by loans from semi-formal 1, informal 1, formal 1, formal 2 and informal 2 sources (3.14 %, 2.26 %, 0.94 %, 0.93 % and 0.58 %, respectively). When we put together all types of borrower transaction costs, which can be expressed in monetary terms under suitable assumptions, semi-formal 2 turns out to be the costliest source of borrowing with 5.70 % transaction cost. The semi-formal 1 with a total transaction cost 3.23 % is the second costliest source. Informal 1 turn out to be having the third highest transaction cost figure of 2.28 %. Commercial banks cum RRBs and cooperatives have a much lower figure of 1.03 % and 1.02 %, respectively. This happens in relative terms when we look upon transaction cost relative to the size of the loan (given in column 2 of Table 5.5). Informal 2 lenders thus continue to have an overall comparative advantage in terms of all transaction costs, which can be expressed in monetary terms.

Table 5.5: Borrower Transaction Cost in Terms of Application, Documentation and Processing Fees Classified by Loan Source

(1)	*(2)*	*(3)*	*(4)*
Loan Sources	*Average Loan Amount Sanctioned in ₹*	*Borrower Search Cost Plus Transaction Cost on Visits to Final Lender as % of Loan Amount Sanctioned*	*Borrower Search Cost Plus Transaction Cost on Visits to Final Lender and on Payment of Various Fees as % of Loan Amount Sanctioned*
Informal-2 (216)	7231.5	0.587	0.59
Informal-1 (50)	10060	2.265	2.28
Semi-formal-2 (20)	11550	3.622	5.70
Semi-formal-1 (63)	5230.2	3.144	3.23
Formal-2 (200)	25752	0.929	1.03
Formal-1 (33)	81409	0.944	1.02

5.3 SUMMARY AND CONCLUSION

In the process of accessing loan from any source, a borrower incurs several types of transaction costs, which can be looked upon as an excess burden on the borrower beyond what he pays to the lender in terms of repayment of the principal with interest. Some of these costs are explicit and some are implicit, and only a few can be expressed in monetary terms to arrive at an overall estimate of borrower transaction cost. Many of the transaction costs, which is rather unobservable, remain outside the orbit of any estimation or analysis. In these circumstances, the present study has attempted to estimate only two types of borrower transaction costs as elaborated below:

- First, the transaction cost which the borrower incurs in terms waiting for sanction and disbursal of loans, commercial banking sector cum RRBs has the worst record of 26.49 days. Cooperative banks come next, involving 10.12 days of waiting on average. Loans from NBFCs involve 10.05 days of waiting, while the traditional rural moneylender takes about 4.50 days to sanction and disburse a loan. SHGs promoted by government/NABARD/NGOs take exactly 8.75 days, while the other informal rural moneylenders like friends, relatives, traders, merchants, shopkeepers, etc. take the minimum amount of time—precisely 2.28 days, to release a loan.
- In terms of monetary transaction cost the borrower incurs in searching for alternatives, approaching the final lender through several trips to him and paying to him in the form of application fees, documentation fees and processing fees, the general presumption is that the informal and semi-formal lenders must be having a strong comparative advantage relative to the formal lending organizations. This presumption is belied by the findings of this study, when the borrower transaction costs are expressed as percentage of the loan amount, in view of the fact that much larger size loan is provided by commercial banks cum RRBs and cooperative banks (about ₹ 81,000 and 25,000, respectively) as compared to the loan size of other lenders (varying between ₹ 5.2 thousand to ₹ 11.5 thousand). Thus, borrower transaction costs turn out to be much less in percentage terms for the first two categories of formal sector lenders (namely, 1.02 % and 1.03 %, respectively) as compared to the two semi-formal sources (3.23 % and 5.70 %, respectively) and the two informal sources (2.28 % and 0.59 %, respectively).

In view of the above-stated findings, it is no surprise that the formal lenders, and especially the commercial banking sector, would not be too keen to provide small loans to a vast number of small borrowers in the country side. The cooperative banks, on the other hand, in spite of their so many off-cited limitations, have been doing this job fairly well—i.e., providing both small and large loans at a relatively low transaction cost to the borrower. The traditional rural moneylender has no easy way to scale up his operations and reduce the transaction cost of his borrower. In fact, the traditional rural moneylender, as long as he enjoys a near-monopoly position in his area of operation, will have little incentive to reduce borrower transaction cost. He can simply pass on this burden to the borrower without inviting a serious loss to his business size. The semi-formal lenders, however, as they are experiencing fierce competition, would be keen to expand their network, besides being keen to provide both small and large loans to minimize their borrower transaction costs (as well as theirs) through economies of scale and scope. This is where there is a contradiction in our policy—while the government talks of financial inclusion through formal financial institution, they are not too keen to make small loans to a large number of borrowers, even though they don't mind moping up all small savings in the form of deposits. The semi-formal sector, which has been expanding at an unprecedented rate over the last one decade or so, is keen to mop up small rural deposits, besides making larger size loans for meeting diversified needs of their borrowers, but they are not being provided the requisite space. The other informal rural lenders, who have strong transaction cost advantages from borrower viewpoint, are making steady progress—often unknown to the knowledge of our policy makers. Given scope and policy support to our cooperatives and the semi-formal sectors, these segments could have easily occupied the space currently being captured by informal lenders, given the fact that our commercial banking sector and RRBs have serious limitations in expanding their domain.

CHAPTER 6

Interlinked Transactions and 'Credit Plus'

6.1 INTRODUCTION

The purpose of this chapter is to assess each loan contract of sample borrowers made during 2009–10 across various sources of credit based on its type i.e., whether interlinked or non-interlinked in nature. Interlinked transaction is one where terms of trade in atleast two markets are jointly determined[1]. This chapter also undertakes a quick review of theoretical as well as empirical literature on the motivations behind choosing a linked transaction over a non-linked one. In the absence of efficient markets in factor services to cope with the problems of seasonality, asymmetric information, non-standard factor services, uncertainty in input supply, adverse price fluctuations and opportunistic behaviour of factor suppliers—all typical of poor agrarian societies—interlinked credit seems to provide a good solution. Several institutions from formal and semi-formal credit sector in India is offering credit under interlinked arrangement by attempting to intervene in multiple markets simultaneously (along with credit), with varying scale, scope and degrees of success, which has been known as 'credit plus' approach.

The rural households are asked against each loan contract whether it was of interlinked nature or, not. Upon an affirmative answer, the respondents were asked whether they were charged any extra fees by the lender to offer the interlinked product, and if so, up to what extent. Respondents were also enquired about the problems faced by them while using the production loan (if any) and how have they handled the same as well as up to what extent they could manage the same. This is basically to identify the role of *Credit plus* service providers in overcoming various risks like production risk, market risk, capacity failure etc, faced by individual borrowers.

---

[1] Basu, K. (1983). The Emergence of Isolation and Interlinkage in Rural Market. Oxford Economic Papers, 35(2), 262–80.

This chapter is organized as follows. In the following section, we offer a brief review of exiting literature on interlinked credit transactions. Section 3 brings out various types of interlinked transactions among the sample villages, which is followed by a section on analysis of 'Credit Plus' transactions. The last section summarizes and concludes the chapter.

6.2 SHORT REVIEW OF LITERATURE

A poor farmer has following credit sources available to him for consumption smoothening: (a) his landlord, in case he is a tenant-farmer; (b) his employer, in whose farm or, household he is employed as a wage labor; (c) trader or, commission agent, to whom he sales his farm produce; (d) trader of consumption goods such as grocery shops, medicine stores, cloth merchants etc.; (e) friends and relatives; (f) local moneylender; and (g) the formal banking system. In case the need extends for production investment the list may not consist of (h), but may include (i) input dealer, from whom he purchases production input and may also seek guidance during pest and disease infestation.

The marketable collateral based lending technology followed by formal financial channel (Datta, 2003)[2] is imbedded with structured norms and procedures (Gill, 2004)[3], rather inflexible repayment schedule (Qureshi, Nabi, and Faruqee, 1996)[4] and mostly caters to production enhancement and diversification needs (Fisher and Sriram, 2002)[5]. Illiterate peasants from lower social strata having small operational land with minimum irrigation potential are the applicant group with least potential to fulfill this matching condition set by formal financial agencies (Sarap, 1990)[6].

Further, loan from formal sources are available during sowing season and least adaptive to borrower's sudden needs (Datta, 1992)[7]. After

---

[2] Datta, S.K. (2003). An Institutional Economics Approach to the Problems of Small Farmer Credit in India. Working Paper 2003–07–01, Ahmedabad: Indian Institute of Management.

[3] Gill, A. (2004). Interlinked Agrarian Credit Markets: Case Study of Punjab. Economic and Political Weekly, 39(33), 3741–3751.

[4] Qureshi, S., Nabi, I. and Faruqee, R.R. (1996). Rural Finance for Growth and Poverty Alleviation. World Bank Policy Research Working Paper No. 1593 (April).

[5] Fisher, T. and Sriram, M.S. (2002). Beyond Micro-credit: Putting Development Back into Micro-Finance, New Delhi: Sage Publications (Vistaar Imprint).

[6] Sarap, K. (1990). Factors Affecting Small Farmers' Access to Institutional Credit in Rural Orissa, India. Development and Change, 21(2,), 281–307.

[7] Datta, S.K. (1992). Understanding Rural Moneylenders—A Study of Two Villages from West Bengal. Study sponsored by NABARD. Ahmedabad: Indian Institute of Management.

experiencing production shocks or other contingences, while a rich borrower would be able to meet his repayment obligations from other resources, a poor farmer may not be able to cope with the same shock/contingencies due to resource constraint (Ray, 1998)[8]. Thus low 'profit potential' poor farmers confronting utmost uncertainty may be either quantity rationed by the supplier or, may be transaction cost rationed by own self.

The poor peasant may also be screened out by professional moneylender due to non-possession of any worthwhile security as demanded by the lender. It is also unexpected that his familiar group would be in a position to extend him considerable financial help for consumption smoothening or, production needs, as they may also belong to same socio-economic strata and exposed to the same type of contingencies. The option now rests on negotiating a credit contract with his landlord, employer or, traders. The situation may lead to some interlinked credit transactions, where terms of trade in at least two markets are determined jointly (Basu, 1983)[9].

At the pre-contractual level of a credit contract, both borrower and lender try to search and look for a matching contractual partner. Lender's action is to hold suitable screening mechanism to avoid *adverse selection*, so as limit the number of 'lemons' in his client set. At the post-contractual stage, lender needs to keep a close watch to prevent any adverse use of fund and monitor whether any post-contractual event has altered borrower's ability and eagerness to repay. Non-payment of dues may be willful in nature, caused by opportunistic behavior by the borrower (known as *moral hazard*). Borrower may also encounter unforeseen shocks as output failures, adverse price fluctuations and/or capacity failures, and may not be able to settle the dues (referred to as *hold up problem*).

Braverman and Guasch (1984)[10] demonstrated that interlinking tenancy with credit contracts would act as a fruitful screening strategy in the rural community. This arrangement is also found to be a strong mechanism for internalizing the post-contractual externalities, i.e., as *moral hazard* (Bardhan, 1989)[11], thus, bringing down the enforcement

---

[8] Ray, D. (1998). Development Economics. New Delhi: Oxford University Press.

[9] Basu, K. (1983). The Emergence of Isolation and Interlinkage in Rural Market. Oxford Economic Papers, 35(2), 262–80.

[10] Braverman, A. and Gausch, J.L. (1984). Capital Requirements, Screening and Interlinked Sharecropping and Credit Contracts. Journal of Development Economics, 14(3), 359–74.

[11] Bardhan, P.K. (1989). A Note on Interlinked Rural Economic Arrangements. In P. Bardhan (ed.) The Economic Theory of Agrarian Institutions (pp. 237–242). Oxford: Clarendon Press.

cost. Also due to repetitive transaction between the same two contracting agents, lender remains assured of loan recovery from the next harvest in case of failure of the standing crop (Gill, 2004)[12]. This kind of arrangement thus also acting as a good mechanism to resolve the *hold up problem.*

The simplest way to apprehend the reasons behind interlinked markets may be to raise the question why in a simple and abstract model of general equilibrium, certain economic agents fall short of practicing the finest form of division of labour and why they don't concentrate on the production of a single commodity. A careful economist's popular answer runs in the presence of either or, both of these factors, (a) economies (diseconomies) of scale and/or scope, and (b) incompleteness or imperfection of markets because of either uncertainty, informational asymmetry or, institutional backwardness of one form or the another. It is interesting to point out that the various alternative explanations attempted so far conceptually boil down to an issue of minimizing transaction costs. This may be a Pareto-efficient move for both the contracting agents.

6.3 TYPES AND EXTENT OF INTERLINKED TRANSACTIONS

In this section, we explain the type of interlinked transactions and the incidences of such transactions (see Table 6.1) observed in the sample villages. It also covers the extent of extra market charge for interlinked service across credit sources (see Table 6.2):

(a) ***Credit-Insurance***: The creditor offers insurance as a bundled deal with credit which may be either of compulsory (pure bundle) or, voluntary (mixed bundle) in nature. This type of interlinking is prevalent among the transactions held with formal and semi-formal sources and predominantly with Banks/RRBs and private NBFCs/ MFIs who offer insurance service as a bundled deal with the basic credit product. In all cases, *credit-insurance* interlinked transaction has turned out to be beneficial for the client group as the borrower could avail insurance at least 3.33 per cent cheaper than the market price. The maximum benefit under this interlinkage has been experienced by the clients of private NBFCs who have availed insurance at a rate around six per cent cheaper than the prevailing market rate.

(b) ***Credit-Land Tenancy***: In this arrangement, landlord offers credit facility to only those who also cultivates his land on lease under rental/share agreement. None of our sample borrower has informed about having this type of interlinked credit transaction.

[12]Ibid.

Table 6.1: Proportion of Different Types of Interlinking Credit Transactions across Lending Agencies

Sources of Credit	*Credit-Insurance*	*Credit-Tenancy*	*Input-Cash*	*Credit-Output*	*Credit-Labor*	*Credit-Extension Service*	*Credit-Emergency Service*	*Credit-Consumable*
Formal-1 (43)	0.14	0	0	0	0	0.00	0.00	0
Formal-2 (193)	0.74	0	0.80	0.46	0	0.94	0.93	0.17
Semiformal-1 (53)	0.03	0	0.08	0	0	0.03	0	0
Semiformal-2 (22)	0.09	0	0.00	0	0	0.03	0	0
Informal-1 (54)	0	0	0.005	0	0.08	0	0	0
Informal-2 (209)	0	0	0.10	0.000	0	0.00	0	0.82

Notes: Formal-1: Commercial Banks and RRB, Formal-2: PACS, Semiformal: MFIs promoted by Govt./NABARD; Semiformal-2: Private MFIs/NBFCs, Informal-1: Money Lender, Informal-2: Grocery Friends/Relatives etc.

Table 6.2: Extra Market Charges (%) for Interlinked Service across Credit Sources

Sources of Credit	*Extra Charge on Insurance*	*Extra Charge on Tenancy*	*Extra Charge on Input Price*	*Extra Charge on Output Price*	*Extra Charge on Labor Sale*	*Extra Charge on Extension Service*	*Extra Charge on Emergency Service*	*Extra Charge on Consumption Goods*
Formal-1 (43)	–4.74 (12)	– (0)	–2 (0)	– (0)	– (0)	0 (0)	0 (1)	– (0)
Formal-2 (193)	–4.97 (12)	– (0)	–4.20 (87)	3.96 (80)	– (0)	–0.34 (35)	–0.59 (33)	–3.63 (0)
Semiformal-1 (53)	–4.43 (7)	– (0)	–4.29 (15)	– (0)	– (0)	– (0)	– (0)	– (0)
Semiformal-2 (22)	–5.30 (11)	– (0)	– (0)	– (0)	– (0)	0 (1)	– (0)	– (0)
Informal-1 (54)	– (0)	– (0)	– (0)	– (0)	–13.75 (2)	– (0)	– (0)	– (0)
Informal-2 (209)	– (0)	– (0)	–3.50 (9)	0 (0)	– (0)	0 (5)	– (0)	7.68 (192)

Note: Figures with negative sign indicate interlinking transaction is cheaper, whereas figures with positive sign indicate the opposite, as compared to the market rate.

(c) ***Input-Credit**:* Lender is an input trader who sells input on credit and recovers his dues after the peasant sells his produce. Highest incidence of such arrangement has been observed in case of multi-purpose PACS, where 87 out of 193 transactions (i.e., 45 per cent) fall under this category, followed by moneylenders who, in 24 out of 54 transactions (i.e., 44 per cent cases) have resorted to such inter-linkage. Upon the usual expectation that this concerted action has increased consumer surplus, farmers have really benefited by accessing input at below market price brought to them by multi-purpose PACS. But the study found instances where rural households have borrowed agricultural input as seeds from friends and relatives at a cheaper rate which is to the same extent as offered by co-operatives. Column 4 of Table 6.2 indicates that informal-2 source has offered input at 3.50 % below the comparable market price as against similar offering from the cooperatives (semiformal-2) which is made available on an average 3.26 % cheaper than market price.

(d) ***Credit-Output**:* Lender is an output trader (commission agent) who offers working capital loan during cultivation in exchange for assured output supply at a pre-determined price. This type of transactions has been primarily observed in the dealings with multipurpose PACS who procure agricultural produce from borrower farmer. Through this arrangement, the farmers on an average have realized around three percent price benefit, in our sample.

(e) ***Credit-Labour**:* Employer-lender lends during the lean period under committed labour supply during the peak period. Our study has found two cases under this arrangement. On average laborers are paid around 14 per cent below the market wage.

(f) ***Credit-Extension**:* Lender makes extension service available to the borrower as a bundled deal with credit which may be either of compulsory (pure bundle) or, voluntary (mixed bundle) in nature. 35 out of a total 193 transactions in cooperatives are reported to be bundled with extension services. The study identifies that multipurpose PACS such as Madhusudankathi (in West Bengal) and Amalsad (in Gujarat) provide free extension service at the borrowers' doorsteps either by arranging extension camps by government agricultural functionaries or, through distribution of leaflets, pamphlets etc. making the service cheaper (as reflected in column 7 of Table 6.2), which otherwise the farmers had to bear in the form of travel expenses, wage loss etc. The institutions thus absorb the cost of accessing the extension service by the rural households.

(g) ***Credit-Emergency Service:*** In case of any post contractual adverse shock which is beyond the borrowers' absorption capacity, which may lead to non-willful default (*hold up problem*), the lender offers further dose of credit. The debt may be in cash as well as consumable for consumption smoothing or, in the form of input to continue the production activity. Such emergency service has been reported by only one cooperative i.e., Amalsad multipurpose PACS, which has offered the service at a price slightly below the market rate.

(h) ***Consumable-Credit:*** Local grocery, cloth merchant, medicine shop etc. offer consumables on credit during lean period and get back the money after harvest. 92 per cent of a total of 209 transactions with local traders have been reported to be interlinked of this type. The arrangement has turned to be on average 11.24 per cent over-priced as compared to pure cash transactions.

6.4 'CREDIT PLUS' APPROACH

The theoretical argument behind wider prevalence of interlinked transactions is the success of such general equilibrium approaches in restoring optimality over the more partial equilibrium approach of focusing merely on credit market imperfections, as followed by majority of the formal banking system. Several institutions in India have been attempting to put this general equilibrium approach into practice by attempting to intervene in several markets simultaneously (along with credit), with varying scale, scope and degrees of success, which has popularly been known as 'credit plus' approach.

Table 6.3 indicates the problems being faced by borrower respondents across sample villages while using production loan. Table 6.4 indicates the extent to which borrowers have handled the problem as mentioned in Table 6.3. Right quality of input and adverse climatic condition evolved as the main problems faced by majority of the borrowers across villages. Among the sample borrowers who faced the problem of right quality of input comes from village Kendri (23%) followed by village Tarpongi (19%), both from the state Chattisgrah. Regarding adverse climatic condition, majority of the affected respondents are from Tarpongi (i.e., 18%) followed by Khulna (i.e., 14%) and Choravidya (i.e., 14%). Except Kotha (only village in Gujarat), respondents of all other sample villages have informed about the problem of right quality of input. Except in Dhusnikhali and Choravidya, borrowers of the rest seven villages have handled the problem and on average have managed moderate profit from the activity.

In Tarpongi and Kendri, the two villages from Chattisgarh, around 80 per cent of the borrowers face the problems of non-availability of right quality and quantity of input. While in Bhatagaon (the third village in Chhattisgarh), the major problem faced by loanee respondents are adverse climatic condition (24 out of 25 borrowers i.e., 96 per cent) and production risk (15 out of 25 borrowers i.e., 60 per cent). On average, borrowers of all three villages of Chhattisgarh have handled those problems to a considerable extent and have realized good profit (with average score above 2).

The prime problem reported by the borrowers in Kotha (the only village selected from Gujarat) is increase in complementary inputs price, which is

Table 6.3: Problems Encountered by Borrowers in Using Loans for Production Activities across Sample Villages

Panel A

(1)	*(2)*	*(3)*	*(4)*	*(5)*	*(6)*	*(7)*	*(8)*
Village	*Right Quality of Input*	*Right Quantity of Input*	*Complementary Input Price Hike*	*Production Risk*	*Managerial Risk*	*Capacity Failure*	*Market Risk*
Tarpongi (42)	35 (20)	32 (32)	13 (14)	16 (13)	13 (16)	7 (16)	11 (13)
Kendri (47)	42 (24)	39 (40)	16 (17)	10 (8)	8 (10)	8 (7)	10 (12)
Bhatagaon (25)	12 (6)	0 (0)	9 (10)	13 (10)	3 (4)	6 (5)	8 (9)
Kotha (46)	0 (0)	1 (1)	21 (23)	11 (9)	13 (16)	14 (12)	14 (16)
Khulna (27)	26 (15)	8 (8)	9 (10)	13 (10)	8 (10)	15 (13)	10 (11)
Dhuchnikhali (25)	21 (12)	7 (7)	7 (8)	19 (15)	9 (11)	15 (13)	7 (8)
Chorabidya (28)	29 (17)	9 (9)	1 (1)	26 (20)	17 (22)	25 (21)	13 (15)
Metiyakhali (27)	3 (2)	1 (1)	10 (11)	12 (10)	1 (1)	20 (17)	1 (1)
Madhusu-dankati (26)	5 (3)	1 (1)	4 (4)	4 (3)	10 (12)	6 (5)	12 (14)
Total	**172 (100)**	**98 (100)**	**90 (100)**	**124 (100)**	**82 (100)**	**116 (100)**	**86 (100)**

Table contd...

Table 6.3 contd...

Panel B

	(9)	(10)	(11)	(12)	(13)	(14)
Village	Storage Problem	Lack of Processing Facility	Transportation Problem	Adverse Climatic Condition	Natural Catastrophe	Adverse Use of Loan
Tarpongi (42)	0 (0)	7 (78)	0 (0)	34 (18)	4 (3)	9 (8)
Kendri (47)	8 (12)	0 (0)	1 (2)	10 (5)	15 (11)	9 (8)
Bhatagaon (25)	2 (3)	0 (0)	0 (0)	22 (12)	10 (7)	7 (6)
Kotha (46)	16 (25)	0 (0)	6 (13)	13 (7)	12 (8)	17 (15)
Khulna (27)	8 (12)	0 (0)	7 (15)	27 (14)	25 (17)	22 (20)
Dhuchni-khali (25)	9 (14)	2 (22)	12 (25)	22 (12)	21 (15)	11 (10)
Chorabidya (28)	12 (19)	0 (0)	20 (42)	28 (15)	29 (20)	18 (16)
Metiyakhali (27)	8 (12)	0 (0)	1 (2)	23 (12)	22 (15)	9 (8)
Madhusu-dankati 26)	1 (2)	0 (0)	0 (0)	7 (4)	4 (3)	10 (8)
Total	**64 (100)**	**9 (100)**	**47 (100)**	**186 (100)**	**142 (100)**	**112 (100)**

Note: Figures in both panels indicate proportion of borrowers reporting such problems. Figures in parentheses indicate the column percentages.

faced by 45 per cent of the loanee respondents followed by storage problem, faced by 36 per cent of the borrowers. On average borrowers have handled those problems and have achieved moderate profit (with average score of 2).

Among the five sample villages from West Bengal, Khulna, Dhusnikhali and Choravidya are worst hit with problems faced in using loans in productive activities, which include problems of right quantity and quality of input, production risk, adverse climatic condition, natural catastrophe and adverse loan use. On the average, the borrowers seem to have handled those problems to some extent and have realized marginal profit (with an average score of around 1.5). In the other two villages, borrowers from Metiyakhali primarily face the problem of capacity failure (76 per cent), adverse climatic condition (84 per cent) and natural catastrophe (84 per cent). In Madhusudankati, the major problem is availability of right quality of input (59 per cent) followed by market risk (50 per cent).

Table 6.4: Indicators of to which Extent Borrowers have handled the Problems, as mentioned in Table 6.3

Panel A

(1)	(2)	(3)	(4)	(5)	(6)	(7)
Village	*Hand 1*	*Hand 2*	*Hand 3*	*Hand 4*	*Hand 5*	*Hand 6*
Tarpongi	2.03 (35)	2.03 (32)	1.84 (13)	2.13 (15)	2.00 (13)	1.00 (7)
Kendri	2.38 (42)	2.07 (49)	1.60 (15)	1.90 (10)	1.75 (8)	1.37 (8)
Bhatagaon	2.00 (11)	– (0)	2.00 (9)	2.15 (13)	2.33 (3)	2.20 (5)
Kotha	– (0)	2.00 (1)	2.00 (20)	2.00 (10)	1.75 (12)	1.78 (14)
Khulna	1.65 (26)	2.00 (8)	1.33 (9)	1.30 (13)	2.00 (8)	1.46 (15)
Dhuchnikhali	1.24 (22)	2.00 (7)	1.28 (7)	1.21 (19)	2.00 (9)	1.53 (15)
Choravidya	1.07 (29)	1.66 (9)	2.00 (1)	1.65 (26)	1.42 (17)	1.16 (25)
Metiyakhali	2.33 (3)	2.00 (1)	1.90 (10)	1.83 (12)	2.00 (1)	1.85 (20)
Madhusudankati	1.80 (5)	1.00 (1)	1.50 (4)	1.00 (4)	1.90 (10)	1.00 (6)

Panel B

	(8)	(9)	(10)	(11)	(12)	(13)	(14)
Village	*Hand7*	*Hand8*	*Hand9*	*Hand10*	*Hand11*	*Hand12*	*Hand13*
Tarpongi	1.81 (11)	– (0)	2.00 (7)	– (0)	1.73 (34)	2.00 (3)	1.88 (9)
Kendri	1.50 (10)	1.25 (8)	– (0)	2.00 (1)	2.00 (10)	2.06 (15)	1.33 (9)
Bhatagaon	2.00 (8)	2.00 (2)	– (0)	– (0)	2.04 (22)	2.00 (10)	1.42 (7)
Kotha	1.92 (14)	2.06 (16)	– (0)	1.33 (6)	1.38 (13)	1.25 (12)	1.93 (16)
Khulna	1.70 (10)	1.33 (9)	– (0)	1.71 (7)	1.07 (26)	1.46 (26)	1.95 (22)
Dhuchni-khali	1.14 (7)	1.55 (9)	1.00 (2)	1.42 (12)	1.68 (22)	1.19 (24)	1.45 (12)
Chorabidya	1.38 (13)	1.58 (12)	– (0)	1.55 (20)	1.25 (28)	1.52 (29)	1.39 (18)
Metiyakhali	2.00 (1)	2.00 (8)	– (0)	2.00 (1)	1.65 (23)	1.50 (22)	1.55 (9)
Madhusu-dankati	1.08 (12)	1.00 (1)	– (0)	– (0)	1.00 (7)	2.25 (4)	1.20 (10)

Notes: Respondents have assigned scores varying from 0 to 3, indicating the extent to which the problem has been handed. 0: not handled at all, leading to maximum loss, 1: leading to moderate loss, 2: handled partially, leading to only moderate profit, 3: handled fully and anticipated profit has been realized. Figures in parentheses indicate the number of respondents facing corresponding problem as mentioned in Table 6.3.

Table 6.5: Indicators of Different Types of Problems Normally faced by the Borrowers while using Loans in Production Activities and how they have handled those Problems

	(1)	(2)	(3)	(4)	(5)	(6)	(7)	(8)	(9)
Problems Type	*Through Individual Effort*	*By Credit Plus Support*	*Help from Neighborhood*	*Help from Govt. Extension Service*	*Private Third Party Intervention*	*Support from NGO/ Voluntary Organization*	*Formal Insurance*	*Number of Borrowers Facing Problem*	*Number of Borrowers not Facing Problem*
Right quality of input	122 (70.93)	13 (7.56)	37 (21.51)	0 (0.00)	0 (0.00)	0 (0.00)	0 (0.00)	172 (100)	117 (40.48)
Right quantity of input	52 (53.06)	10 (10.42)	35 (36.41)	0 (0.00)	0 (0.00)	0 (0.00)	0 (0.00)	98 (100)	190 (65.97)
Complementary input price hike	80 (90.91)	6 (6.82)	0 (0.00)	0 (0.00)	0 (0.00)	2 (2.27)	0 (0.00)	88 (100)	196 (68.53)
Production risk	95 (78.51)	14 (11.57)	4 (3.31)	1 (0.83)	0 (0)	2 (1.65)	5 (4.13)	121 (100)	165 (56.79)
Managerial risk	46 (55.42)	27 (32.53)	10 (12.05)	0 (0.00)	0 (0.00)	0 (0.00)	0 (0.00)	83 (100)	205 (71.43)
Capacity failure	86 (75.44)	20 (17.54)	8 (7.02)	0 (0.00)	0 (0.00)	0 (0.00)	0 (0.00)	114 (100)	171 (59.68)
Market risk	50 (57.47)	32 (36.78)	1 (1.15)	1 (1.15)	1 (1.15)	2 (2.30)	0 (0.00)	87 (100)	200 (69.93)
Storage problem	43 (68.25)	9 (14.29)	11 (17.46)	0 (0.00)	0 (0.00)	0 (0.00)	0 (0.00)	63 (100)	227 (77.78)
Lack of processing Facility	4 (44.44)	3 (33.33)	2 (22.22)	0 (0.00)	0 (0.00)	0 (0.00)	0 (0.00)	9 (100)	278 (96.86)
Transportation problem	38 (80.85)	4 (8.51)	5 (10.64)	0 (0.00)	0 (0.00)	0 (0.00)	0 (0.00)	47 (100)	240 (83.62)
Adverse climatic condition	120 (65.57)	22 (12.02)	17 (9.29)	1 (0.55)	16 (8.74)	7 (3.83)	0 (0.00)	183 (100)	102 (35.42)
Natural catastrophe	25 (17.36)	10 (6.94)	8 (5.56)	1 (0.69)	0 (0.00)	87 (60.42)	13 (9.03)	144 (100)	142 (50.00)
Adverse use of loan	59 (53.64)	5 (4.55)	13 (11.02)	0 (0.00)	0 (0.00)	33 (30.00)	0 (0.00)	110 (100)	176 (61.32)
Total	**820 (62.17)**	**176 (13.34)**	**151 (11.44)**	**4 (0.003)**	**17 (1.30)**	**133 (10.08)**	**18 (13.64)**	**1319 (100)**	

Note: Figures outside parentheses indicate numbers of cases, while those in parentheses indicate row percentages except for column 9 which represents column % of borrowers not facing this problem.

While the first problem is moderately handled by borrowers with the help of their cooperatives, they are apparently not able to handle the second problem to their satisfaction.

Table 6.5 provides a cumulative picture of various problems being faced by 302 borrower respondents (among a total of 350 sample households) while using production loan, besides indicating how they have handled those problems. This would help us to assess the importance of 'Credit Plus' provider in the borrower's production activity. It is evident from Table 6.5 that individual effort evolves as the single most important way to handle the range of problems faced while utilizing the production loan. Though support from 'credit plus' provider comes as second best solution, its importance in front of individual effort looks insignificant. Against 814 problem cases out of a total of 1309 (i.e., 62.18 %), where borrowers have resorted to individual effort to handle the problems, support from 'credit plus' provider is found to be helpful in only 173 cases (i.e., 13.22 %) followed by help from neighbors in 150 cases (i.e., 11.46 %).

Table 6.5 also highlights that the prime problems as identified in the earlier paragraph is primarily addressed by the borrowers through their individual effort. For problem faced by the borrowers due to natural catastrophe, the service provided by NGO is really notable (around 61 per cent of borrowers). Prominence of 'Credit Plus' approach is observed is addressing market risk, followed by managerial risk and adverse climatic condition. Among the 86 borrowers who faced market risk 31 (i.e., 36 per cent) had resorted to 'Credit Plus' provider. Among the 83 borrowers who faced managerial risk 27 (i.e., 33 per cent) again availed the support of 'Credit Plus' provider. 'Credit Plus' support was also of help to 12 per cent borrowers who faced adverse climatic conditions. Help from neighborhoods turned out to be of great help in availing input in right quality as well as in right quantity.

6.5 SUMMARY AND CONCLUSION

In the process of availing a loan, a borrower often chooses between an interlinked and non-interlinked transaction. In case of interlinked transaction, the terms of trade in at least two markets are simultaneously determined. The traditional argument behind such interlinked transaction is lenders' exercise of monopoly power over the vulnerable poor borrowers, while a more modern institutional approach highlights the lower transaction cost benefit derived by both lenders and borrowers through interlinked dealings as against non-linked transactions. While majority of lenders from formal sector credit follow a minimalist credit approach, few new generation semiformal institutions (i.e., MFIs) as well as multipurpose cooperative societies are offering credit as well as some complementary services i.e., a multimarket intervention popularly known as 'credit plus' approach. In these circumstances, the present study has attempted to identify the nature and extent of interlinked transactions across lenders and up to what extent 'credit plus' approach has been successful to fill in the lacuna (if any) left out by its minimalist counterpart:

1. Input-cash, credit-output and consumable cash have evolved as the most important interlinked transactions in our study. While the former two were mostly found under formal-2 (precisely, under multipurpose PACS), consumable-credit is found to be a common incidence in cases of local traders like cloth merchants, grocery or medical shop-keepers, etc.
2. Through both credit-input and credit-output interlinking arrangements, the farmers on an average have realized around three percent price benefit. On the contrary, consumable-credit interlinking, which is mostly in the private domain has turned to be on average 11.24 per cent over-priced against cash transaction.
3. Even though interlinked credit is often looked upon as undesirable and coming in the way of promoting equity and livelihood improvement, the study finds that interlinked credit extended even under informal credit sector has succeeded in evolving appropriate strategies to handle rural credit market failure.
4. Availability of right quality of input, adverse climatic condition and natural catastrophe turn out be most important problems faced by borrowers while utilizing production loan.
5. In most cases, borrowers had to resort to individual effort in addressing various problems in production followed by help from 'credit plus' provider and support from neighbor.
6. It is observed that the three villages of West Bengal, namely, Khulna, Dhusnikhali and Choravidya where borrowers have reported maximum problems in using production loan are the villages under 'minimalist credit'. On the contrary, the two villages which seem to have handled most of the problems and to a considerable extent are Madhusudankati of West Bengal and Kotha of Gujarat, are under the service area of strong 'Credit Plus' providers in the form of well-functioning cooperatives.

CHAPTER 7

Probing Extension Services in the Context of Rural Credit

7.1 INTRODUCTION

One might wonder why all of a sudden towards the end of this study on rural credit we feel the urge to probe the nature, extent and effectiveness of extension services. It is important to answer this question before proceeding further. Any credit transaction, as we have explained earlier, has the three-fold problems of (i) adverse selection, (ii) moral hazard or opportunism, and (iii) locking-in effect, from the viewpoint of both the parties. The first problem arises before a credit is offered, while the other two problems arise afterwards. Given the fact that a credit contract can't standalone, an act of trust either in the form of acceptable collateral or a credit-worthy project must be submitted by the borrower for lender's scrutiny and verification, and thus to win over the lender's confidence. Credit being a transaction over a period of time, rather than at a point in time, this scrutiny, verification and possible corrections in the credit-sponsored project must occur over time. This is where the role of extension creeps in. Moreover, as long as extension and monitoring go almost hand in hand, the tasks of extension and monitoring are often performed simultaneously. In our attempt to probe the role of extension in this chapter, we shall assume that an extension agency can perform the task of monitoring as well, at almost an insignificant marginal cost. For example, if good extension data are maintained over time not only on the extension inputs to the borrower's project, but also on effective use of such inputs, these records can be utilized in future to separate out 'good' borrowers from 'bad' ones, thus resolving the adverse selection problem from a lender's viewpoint. At the same time, a rigorous extension service coupled with monitoring can also put a check on opportunistic behavior of the borrower, besides saving the borrower's project under adverse contingent situations through supply of good advice and monitoring. Thus, extension, if interpreted in this broader sense, has the potential to resolve—at least to some extent, all the three fundamental problems affecting credit or causing credit market failures. There is also another dimension to the role of good extension services in the context of credit. By at least partially resolving the above-stated problems of credit, it can boost up the lender's supply of credit, while in the longer run boosting up demand from genuine borrowers. In fact, a good extension service has thus potential to improve performance of not only household credit, but also credit for collective/societal projects. For example, a good extension service on sanitation can not only create more awareness and thus boost up societal demand, but also, through creation of better awareness-induced monitoring, provide a stronger impetus to the society's willingness to meet the increased demand. These roles of extension services become all the more important in rural settings, which are often marred by market imperfections and market failures on various fronts. It is against this conceptual background we find it important to examine the various dimensions of extension services and their effectiveness in the judgment of sample borrowers.

This chapter is organized as follows. Section 2 brings out the extent of borrowers' familiarity with official extension services on agriculture, veterinary and fisheries, while at the same time reporting average annual expenditure incurred by the borrowers on extension and follow up action. Section 3 assesses the importance of different sources of extension information from the viewpoints of sample borrowers. Sections 4 and 5 bring out the effectiveness of different types of extension services in agriculture and allied activities, respectively. Sections 6 and 7 highlight the effectiveness of extension services on group formation and on general extension services, respectively. The final section summarizes and concludes this chapter.

7.2 BORROWERS' FAMILIARITY WITH AND AVERAGE ANNUAL EXPENSES ON OFFICIAL EXTENSION SERVICES ON AGRICULTURE, VETERINARY AND FISHERIES

Panels A and B of Table 7.1 describe the borrower's familiarity with official extension service in the form of an index varying between 0 and 3, besides reporting borrower's annual expenditure on extension and follow up actions. Panel A reports these figures for all observations, whereas Panel B reports these figures for only those borrowers who have incurred positive expenditure in utilizing extension services. Three types of extension services are considered—those related to agriculture, veterinary and fishery. From panel A, it is observed that out of all sample households (350), as many as 315 have expressed interest in agriculture, whereas

Table 7.1: Familiarity with Official Extension Service and Approximate Annual Expenditure Thereon across Activities

Panel A: Averages for All Observations Engaged in Relevant Activities

(1)	*(2)*	*(3)*	*(4)*	*(5)*	*(6)*	*(7)*
Activity Type	*Index of Familiarity in Agriculture (0–3)*	*Annual Expenditure on Extension in Agriculture*	*Index of Familiarity in Veterinary (0–3)*	*Annual Expenditure in ₹ on Extension in Veterinary*	*Index of Familiarity in Fisheries (0–3)*	*Annual Expenditure in ₹ on Extension in Fisheries*
Agriculture (315)	0.85 (116.40)	677 (238.20)	0.70 (122.4)	175 (388)	0.05 (391)	50 (816.60)
Animal husbandry (250)	0.80 (115.08)	711 (247.40)	0.80 (120)	207 (378.40)	0.07 (380.60)	62 (796)
Fisheries (48)	0.60 (153.40)	275 (363.20)	0.60 (112)	130 (283.40)	0.30 (157.40)	310 (354.70)

Panel B: Averages for Observations Incurring Positive Annual Expenditure

(1)	*(2)*	*(3)*	*(4)*	*(5)*	*(6)*	*(7)*
Activity Type	*Extent of Familiarity (Agriculture)*	*Approx Annual Expenditure (Agriculture)*	*Extent of Familiarity (Veterinary)*	*Approx Annual Expenditure (Veterinary)*	*Extent of Familiarity (Fishery)*	*Approx Annual Expenditure (Fishery)*
Agriculture (104)	1.70 (47.36)	2053 (114)	1.05 (103)	275 (302.5)	0.04 (533)	75 (771.50)
Animal husbandry (73)	1.20 (86.30)	1852 (141)	2 (41.4)	710 (187)	0.07 (444.20)	77 (761)
Fisheries (6)	0.70 (182)	83 (245)	0.30 (155)	428 (184)	1 (0)	2050 (89.30)

Note: Figures in parentheses represent number of observations for the first column and the value of CV for other columns, respectively, in both panels of this table.

250 in animal husbandry, and only 48 in fisheries. This shows the relative significance of these three activities among the sample borrowers. However, it may be noted that these interest groups are not mutually exclusive. The moment we concentrate on borrowers incurring positive expenditure on extension services in these three fields, the size of the interest groups come down rapidly from 315 to 104 for agriculture, from 250 to 73 for animal husbandry, and from 48 to 6 for fisheries. Thus, we see that a large number of borrowers look up on extension as a free service i.e., they don't want to spend any money in procuring extension services nor in undertaking follow up actions, which will cost them some amount of money. This means that value of official extension services is too low in the minds of sample borrowers, given lack of awareness, on the one hand, and poor quality of government extension services, on the other. It appears that unless and until effective private extension services appear on the scene, neither awareness will grow, nor the quality of government extension services will improve competitive pressure. If we consider all relevant borrower groups, the indices of familiarity with government official extension services in these three fields are 0.85, 0.80 and 0.30 for groups practicing agriculture, animal husbandry and fishery, respectively. The average annual expenditure incurred by these three prime groups are, respectively, ₹ 677, ₹ 207 and ₹ 310. It may be noted that both familiarity indices and annual expenditure figures are far lower for other groups (e.g., for an agriculturist for veterinary or fishery). The same things also holds true in panel B, which reports average figures for borrowers incurring positive expenditure on official extension services in these three fields. The familiarity indices shoot up to 1.7, 2 and 1, respectively, for interest groups of borrowers engaged in agriculture, animal husbandry and fishery, respectively, who are incurring positive expenses. The average annual expenditure on extension by these three groups also rise significantly from ₹ 677 to ₹ 2055 for agriculturist borrowers, from ₹ 207 to ₹ 710 for borrowers with major interest in animal husbandry, and from ₹ 310 to ₹ 2050 for those having strong interest in fishery. There is however high degree of variability in reported figures in these two panels, as can be seen from the high values of coefficients of variation, as reported within parentheses in each cell of these two panels.

7.3 IMPORTANCE OF DIFFERENT SOURCES OF EXTENSION INFORMATION

Tables 7.2A to 7.2C highlight the importance of different sources of extension information, as attached by the sample borrowers. Importance

Table 7.2A: Importance of Different Sources of Extension Information Related to Size of Operational Holding of Sample Households

Operational Landholding Class of Households	*Indices of Importance (0–1) by Source*									
	News Papers	*Extension Bulletins*	*Newsletters/ Magazines*	*Production Guidelines*	*Personal Letters from Extension Agents*	*Opinion Leaders/Progressive Farmers*	*Neighbors/ Friends/ Relatives*	*Farmers' Club*	*Radio*	*Television*
Landless (33)	0.66	0.12	0.21	0.03	0.09	0.27	0.60	0.33	0.60	0.45
Small (274)	0.70	0.13	0.16	0.03	0.01	0.26	0.73	0.28	0.60	0.60
Large (43)	0.86	0.28	0.30	0.02	0.02	0.44	0.76	0.28	0.58	0.86
Overall (350)	0.72	0.15	0.18	0.02	0.02	0.28	0.72	0.28	0.60	0.61

Note: Figures in parentheses represent number of observations.

Table 7.2B: Importance of Different Sources of Extension Information Related to Extent of Familiarity to Important Village Personnel of Sample Households

Extent of Familiarity of Households	*Indices of Importance (0–1) by Source*									
	News Papers	*Extension Bulletins*	*News Letters/ Magazines*	*Production Guidelines*	*Personal Letters from Extension Agents*	*Opinion Leaders/Progressive Farmers*	*Neighbors/ Friends/ Relatives*	*Farmers' Club*	*Radio*	*Television*
Nil (31)	0.20	0.00	0.00	0.00	0.00	0.10	0.60	0.60	0.32	0.67
Moderate (16)	0.38	0.12	0.00	0.06	0.00	0.18	0.73	0.20	0.50	0.56
High (303)	0.80	0.17	0.21	0.02	0.02	0.30	0.72	0.31	0.63	0.61
Overall (350)	0.72	0.15	0.18	0.02	0.02	0.28	0.72	0.28	0.60	0.61

Note: Figures in parentheses represent number of observations.

Table 7.2C: Importance of Different Sources of Extension Information Related to Savings and Insurance Status of Sample Households

Savings and Insurance Status of Sample Households	*Indices of Importance (0–1) by Source*									
	News Papers	*Extension Bulletins*	*Newsletters /Magazines*	*Production Guidelines*	*Personal Letters from Extension Agents*	*Opinion Leaders/Progressive Farmers*	*Neighbors/ Friends/ Relatives*	*Farmers' Club*	*Radio*	*Television*
Nil (54)	0.65	0.11	0.12	0.04	0.02	0.22	0.06	0.24	0.51	0.50
Only savings (109)	0.65	0.11	0.09	0.009	0.009	0.22	0.80	0.30	0.60	0.50
Only insurance (25)	0.80	0.16	0.08	0.00	0.04	0.24	0.64	0.16	0.65	0.72
Both (162)	0.80	0.20	0.27	0.03	0.04	0.35	0.76	0.32	0.61	0.64
Overall (350)	0.72	0.15	0.18	0.02	0.02	0.28	0.72	0.28	0.60	0.61

Note: Figures in parentheses represent number of observations.

of various extension information sources is represented by average values of a binary variable (0 or 1), depending up on whether a borrower makes use of a particular source or not. The average values of these binary variables, as reported in these three tables, therefore, represent the proportions of borrower households tapping any particular source. Table 7.2A to 7.2C relate the indices of importance (i.e., proportions) to three important attributes—namely, borrower's operational holding size, their extent of familiarity to important village personnel and their savings and insurance status, respectively. From the last row of each of these tables, one can see that the sample borrowers attach high importance to newspapers, neighbors/friends/relatives, television and radio as most commonly used sources of extension information with their importance indices as 0.72, 0.72, 0.61 and 0.60, respectively. Opinion leaders/ progressive farmers and farmer's club come next with importance index of 0.28 each. The importance of extension bulletins and newsletter/ magazines is moderately low (their indices being 0.15 and 0.18, respectively), whereas production guidelines and personal letters from extension agents have very little significance (with their importance index being 0.02 each).

A careful look at these three tables also tends to give an impression that these importance or use indices of extension have a bias in favor of larger holding groups, except in cases of production guidelines, farmer's club and radio (Table 7.2A). This bias is also seen in favor of borrower households having high degree of familiarity to important village personnel, except for production guidelines, farmer's club and television (Table 7.2B). Table 7.2C displays some bias in favor of borrower groups having insurance/both insurance and savings, except for sources like production guidelines, neighbors/friends/relatives, radio and television. Obviously, there is immense room for improvement of extension education, especially through channels like production bulletin, neighbors, farmer's club, radio and television network.

7.4 EFFECTIVENESS OF DIFFERENT TYPES OF EXTENSION SERVICES IN AGRICULTURE

Tables 7.3A to 7.3E describe effectiveness indices of different types of extension services in agriculture. This effectiveness index is also measured as proportion of borrower households having benefited from a particular form of extension service. Table 7.3A describes variations in this index across extension types and sample villages. The major findings in this context are as follows. There are large variations in this index across rows

Table 7.3A: Effectiveness of Different Types of Extension Service in Agriculture (0–1) across Sample Villages

Village	*Introduction to New/ Improved/High Yielding Crop Variety*	*Improved Agronomic Practices*	*Fertilizer Application*	*Soil and Water Conservation*	*Insect Control and Pesticide Application*	*Awareness about Machinery Use*	*Disease and Parasite Control*	*Post-Harvest Technology*
Bhatagaon (40)	0.72	0.24	0.42	0.16	0.61	0.00	0.18	0.06
Kendri (50)	0.50	0.04	0.90	0.60	0.64	0.04	0.54	0.30
Tarpongi (46)	0.20	0.02	0.13	0.10	0.43	0.20	0.43	0.21
Chorabidya (24)	0.95	0.63	0.90	0.50	0.90	0.04	0.10	0.10
Dhuchnikhali (29)	1.00	0.40	1.00	0.31	0.90	0.06	0.30	0.06
Khulna (28)	1.00	0.30	1.00	0.70	0.90	0.00	0.40	0.07
Metiyakhali (24)	0.20	0.30	0.40	0.60	0.20	0.50	0.30	0.30
Madhusudankati (30)	0.90	0.30	0.90	0.95	0.95	0.03	0.93	0.03
Kotha (44)	0.93	0.30	0.80	0.80	0.80	0.80	0.90	0.80

Note: Figures in parentheses represent number of observations.

Table 7.3B: Effectiveness of Different Types of Extension Service in Agriculture (0–1) Related to Operational Holding Status of Sample Households

Operational Holding Status of Sample Households	*Effectiveness Indices (0–1) by Types of Extension Service in Agriculture*							
	Introduction to New/Improved/ High Yielding Crop Variety	*Improved Agronomic Practices*	*Fertilizer Application*	*Soil and Water Conservation*	*Insect Control and Pesticide Application*	*Awareness about Machinery Use*	*Disease and Parasite Control*	*Post-Harvest Technology*
Small (272)	0.70	0.30	0.70	0.50	0.70	0.20	0.50	0.21
Large (43)	0.72	0.12	0.70	0.60	0.80	0.40	0.70	0.40
overall (315)	0.70	0.24	0.70	0.50	0.70	0.20	0.50	0.24

Note: Figures in parentheses represent number of observations.

Table 7.3C: Effectiveness of Different Types of Extension Service in Agriculture (0–1) Related to Extent of Familiarity to Important Village/Local Personnel of Sample Households

Extent of Familiarity of Households	*Effectiveness Indices (0–1) by Types of Extension Service in Agriculture*							
	Introduction to New/Improved/ High Yielding Crop Variety	*Improved Agronomic Practices*	*Fertilizer Application*	*Soil and Water Conservation*	*Insect Control and Pesticide Application*	*Awareness about Machinery Use*	*Disease and Parasite Control*	*Post-Harvest Technology*
Nil (31)	0.80	0.25	0.50	0.08	0.70	0.00	0.16	0.04
Moderate (16)	0.44	0.06	0.43	0.31	0.50	0.20	0.20	0.20
High (303)	0.80	0.25	0.80	0.60	0.70	0.20	0.54	0.30

Note: Figures in parentheses represent number of observations.

Table 7.3D: Effectiveness of Different Types of Extension Service in Agriculture (0–1) Related to Status of Holding of Agricultural Equipment of Sample Households

Status of Holding of Agricultural Equipment of Sample Households	*Effectiveness Indices (0–1) by Types of Extension Service in Agriculture*							
	Introduction to New/Improved/ High Yielding Crop Variety	*Improved Agronomic Practices*	*Fertilizer Application*	*Soil and Water Conservation*	*Insect Control and Pesticide Application*	*Awareness about Machinery Use*	*Disease and Parasite Control*	*Post-Harvest Technology*
Nil (163)	0.70	0.20	0.70	0.50	0.70	0.10	0.50	0.20
Less equipped (73)	0.73	0.23	0.74	0.40	0.80	0.04	0.40	0.20
Well equipped (79)	0.70	0.20	0.62	0.50	0.70	0.13	0.50	0.30

Note: Figures in parentheses represent number of observations.

Table 7.3E: Effectiveness of Different Types of Extension Service in Agriculture (0–1) Related to Maximum Educational Status of Adult Males in Sample Households

Educational Status	*Effectiveness Indices (0–1) by Types of Extension Service in Agriculture*							
	Introduction to New/Improved/ High Yielding Crop Variety	*Improved Agronomic Practices*	*Fertilizer Application*	*Soil and Water Conservation*	*Insect Control and Pesticide Application*	*Awareness about Machinery Use*	*Disease and Parasite Control*	*Post-Harvest Technology*
Illiterate (20)	0.60	0.20	0.50	0.15	0.65	0.10	0.20	0.20
Literate (83)	0.70	0.42	0.72	0.50	0.80	0.13	0.33	0.16
Up to SSC (132)	0.60	0.20	0.80	0.60	0.70	0.10	0.54	0.20
Above SSC (80)	0.80	0.20	0.80	0.60	0.70	0.45	0.70	0.50

Note: Figures in parentheses represent number of observations.

under each column, thus indicating strong variation in performances across the sample villages. For example, the first three villages from the top (all belonging to Chhattisgarh) are pretty weak in almost all aspects of agricultural extension except Bhatagaon in introduction of HYV crops, and Kendri in fertilizer application, soil and water conservation, and disease and parasite control. The next four villages of West Bengal, which are located within Indian Sundarbans seem to be weak in disease and parasite control, in use of post-harvest technology, and in creating awareness about machinery use (except Metiyakhali). This village of Metiyakhali, in spite of existence of a fairly well functioning-LAMPS, has demonstrated weaknesses in application of HYV varieties, following improved agronomics practices, in fertilizer applications and insect control and pesticide application. The two villages of Dhuchnikhali and Khulna seem to have done very well in application of HYV, fertilizer application and insect control cum pesticide application, and moderately well in improved agronomic practices and soil-water conservation—thanks to the existence of an NGO called Youth Development center. The village of Choravidya—partly because of its locational advantage on the two sides of a main road and existence of an NBFC, seems to have done pretty well in all other aspects of agricultural extension. The villages of Madhusudankati from West Bengal and Kotha from South Gujarat have well known multipurpose cooperatives, resulting in excellent performance in almost all aspects of agricultural extension except for low awareness about machinery use and use of post-harvest technology in Madhusudankati.

Tables 7.3B to 7.3E relate effectiveness of agricultural extension to borrower attributes like size group of holding, familiarity to important village personnel, agricultural equipment holding status and educational status of adult males, respectively. Table 7.3B shows bias in favor of larger landholding group, except in case of improved agronomic practices. A similar pattern is true in favor of borrower households having strong familiarity to important village personnel, except with respect to application of HYV seeds, improved agronomic practices and insect control (Table 7.3C). Table 7.3D shows some bias in favor of better equipped households in terms of agricultural equipment, in almost all spheres of agriculture extension except soil-water conservation and disease cum parasite control. Table 7.3E, too shows some bias in favor of relatively better educated households in terms of application of HYV seeds, fertilizer, soil-water conservation measures, machineries, disease cum parasite control and post-harvest technology.

7.5 EFFECTIVENESS OF DIFFERENT TYPES OF EXTENSION SERVICES IN ALLIED ACTIVITIES

Tables 7.4A to 7.4C judge effectiveness of different types of extension services in allied agricultural activities among the sample households. The different types of allied activities considered in this context are cattle/sheep/goat/poultry production, animal vaccination, their de-worming, their health checkup, their pregnancy checkup, artificial insemination, external parasite spray, use of Azolla/silage/mineral mix in animal feed, and fishery, poultry, duckery or sericultural production. Once again the proportion of borrower households interested in allied agricultural activities, who have made use of different specific forms of extension service in this regard are used as crude measures of effectiveness index. In Table 7.4A, these effectiveness indices are classified across villages and service categories. Once again, there is high degree of variation across sample villages. While extension services on cattle/sheep/goat production, vaccination, health checkup, pregnancy checkup and external parasite spray are being used to some extent in all the villages, this is not true of other services like de-worming, artificial insemination, use of Azolla etc. and production of fishery, poultry, duckery and sericulture. The maximum order of de-worming is observed in the village of Tarpongi in Chhattisgarh, whereas it is not at all used in Choravidya and Khulna, and almost insignificantly in Kendri, Dhuchnikhali and Kotha. Again, artificial insemination is effective only in 16% to 20% cases in the two co-operatively strong villages of Madhusudankati and Kotha; it is non-existent or relatively insignificant in other villages. Use of Azolla etc. in animal feed is observed to some extent (16% to 20%) in the two villages of Metiyakhali and Madhusudankati, but it is non-existent or relatively insignificant in other villages. Fisheries extension is used to some extent in the villages of Madhusudankati, Choravidya and Metiyakhali (20% to 65%), but it is negligible in other villages. Use of extension on poultry, duckery and sericulture is observed to some extent only in the two villages of Khulna and Metiyakhali.

These crude indices of effectiveness of extension services in allied agricultural activities seem to have an upward bias only with respect to cattle/sheep/goat production, vaccination, health checkup and pregnancy checkup, but not with respect to other extension services under allied agricultural activities (Table 7.4B). These indices also seem to have a bias in favor of borrower households with strong order of familiarity to locally important personnel, but this is not true of extension services with respect to de-worming, fishery and duckery (Table 7.4C).

Table 7.4A: Effectiveness of Different Types of Extension Services in Allied Agricultural Activities across Sample Villages

	Effectiveness Indices (0–1) by Types of Extension Service in Allied Agriculture											
Village	*Cattle/ Sheep/ Goat Production*	*Vaccination*	*De-Worming*	*Health Checkup*	*Pregnancy Checkup*	*Artificial Insemination*	*External Parasite Spray*	*Use of Azolla/ Silage/ Mineral Mix*	*Fishery*	*Poultry*	*Duckery*	*Sericulture*
Bhatagaon	0.06	0.73	0.13	0.13	0.20	0.06	0.13	0.00	0.00	0.00	0.00	0.00
Kendri	0.90	0.90	0.02	0.72	0.31	0.04	0.36	0.00	0.06	0.00	0.00	0.00
Tarpongi	0.90	0.95	0.40	0.60	0.20	0.00	0.40	0.00	0.00	0.00	0.00	0.00
Chorabidya	0.20	0.96	0.00	0.93	0.96	0.00	0.96	0.03	0.36	0.06	0.00	0.00
Dhuchnikhali	0.10	0.90	0.03	1.00	0.90	0.03	0.72	0.10	0.10	0.06	0.00	0.03
Khulna	0.60	0.95	0.00	0.93	0.96	0.00	0.48	0.03	0.06	0.24	0.30	0.30
Metiyakhali	0.80	0.65	0.20	0.80	0.60	0.10	0.13	0.20	0.65	0.62	0.24	0.10
Madhusudankati	0.17	1.00	0.20	1.00	1.00	0.16	0.60	0.16	0.20	0.00	0.00	0.00
Kotha	0.76	0.84	0.02	0.84	0.80	0.20	0.30	0.02	0.02	0.00	0.00	0.00

Table 7.4B: Effectiveness of Different Types of Extension Services in Allied Agricultural Activities Related to Maximum Educational Status of Adult Males in Sample Households

Educational Status	*Effectiveness Indices (0–1) by Types of Extension Service in Allied Agriculture*											
	Cattle/ Sheep/Goat Production	*Vaccination*	*De-Worming*	*Health Checkup*	*Pregnancy Checkup*	*Artificial Insemination*	*External Parasite Spray*	*Use of Azolla/Silage /Mineral Mix*	*Fishery*	*Poultry*	*Duckery*	*Sericulture*
Illiterate (17)	0.60	0.70	0.13	0.80	0.60	0.06	0.53	0.06	0.20	0.30	0.13	0.00
Literate (72)	0.41	0.90	0.20	0.80	0.75	0.50	0.50	0.11	0.20	0.20	0.04	0.02
SSC (110)	0.80	0.92	0.07	0.73	0.05	0.02	0.41	0.03	0.20	0.10	0.02	0.02
Above SSC (64)	0.75	0.90	0.08	0.90	0.80	0.15	0.41	0.05	0.06	0.01	0.01	0.01

Note: Figures in parentheses represent number of observations.

Table 7.4C: Effectiveness of Different Types of Extension Services in Allied Agricultural Activities with Respect to Extent of Familiarity to Village/Local Personnel

Famili-arity	*Effectiveness Indices (0–1) by Types of Extension Service in Allied Agriculture*											
	Cattle/ Sheep/Goat Production	*Vaccination*	*De-Worming*	*Health Checkup*	*Pregnancy Checkup*	*Artificial Insemination*	*External Parasite Spray*	*Use of Azolla/ Silage /Mineral Mix*	*Fishery*	*Poultry*	*Duckery*	*Sericulture*
Very Weak (8)	0.10	0.60	0.14	0.30	0.20	0.00	0.30	0.00	0.00	0.00	0.00	0.00
Medium (11)	0.50	0.60	0.00	0.50	0.50	0.10	0.10	0.00	0.20	0.10	0.10	0.00
Good (244)	0.60	0.90	0.10	0.80	0.60	0.10	0.50	0.10	0.10	0.10	0.02	0.02

Note: Figures in parentheses represent number of observations.

7.6 EFFECTIVENESS OF EXTENSION SERVICES ON GROUP FORMATION AMONG BORROWERS

As formation of peer group of borrowers is a critical instrument to make apparently credit-deprived borrowers credit-worthy, questions are asked to relevant borrowers about use of different types of extension services with by such groups. The relevant extension services in this context are group formation, setting up norms of behavior, leadership training, imparting knowledge of book-keeping, creating bank-SHG linkage and organizing federations of SHGs. Use of these extension services is reported in Tables 7.5A to 7.5E. Once again the proportion of relevant borrower households making use of the above stated extension services are crudely looked up on as indices of effectiveness of these services. In cooperatively most strong village of Kotha in Gujarat, SHGs are non-existent, though there seems to be enough room for SHG formation among landless households, to achieve an inclusive process of growth. However, in the other two villages with relatively well-functioning co-operatives—namely, Metiyakhali and Madhusudankati of West Bengal, these extension services seem to have already made some dent. This is also true of three group related extension services—namely, group formation, setting up norms of behavior and linking SHGs to banks

Table 7.5A: Effectiveness of Different Types of Extension Services on Group (SHG, PG, JLG) Formation in Households across Sample Villages

Village Name	*Effectiveness Indices (0–1) by Types of Extension Service in Allied Agriculture*					
	Formation of Self-Help Groups	*Creation of Norms of Behavior*	*Leadership Development*	*Knowledge of Book-Keeping*	*Help in SHG-Bank Link*	*Link with Higher Tier/Fed*
Bhatagaon (50)	0.34	0.32	0.08	0.00	0.02	0.00
Kendri (50)	0.30	0.12	0.04	0.10	0.10	0.00
Tarpongi (50)	0.18	0.04	0.02	0.02	0.08	0.00
Choravidya (30)	0.56	0.76	0.03	0.00	0.80	0.00
Dhuchnikhali (30)	0.66	0.40	0.06	0.06	0.53	0.00
Khulna (50)	0.86	0.56	0.03	0.00	0.80	0.00
Madhusudankati (30)	0.56	0.00	0.00	0.30	0.50	0.06
Metiyakhali (30)	0.76	0.73	0.50	0.26	0.50	0.10
Kotha (50)	0.00	0.00	0.00	0.00	0.00	0.00

Note: Figures in parentheses indicate the number of observations.

Table 7.5B: Effectiveness of Different Types of Extension Services on Group (SHG, PG, JLG) Formation with Respect to Operational Holding Status of Sample Households

Operational Landholding Class	*Effectiveness Indices (0–1) by Types of Extension Service in Allied Agriculture*					
	Formation of Self-Help Groups	*Creation of Norms of Behavior*	*Leadership Development*	*Knowledge of Book-Keeping*	*Help in SHG-Bank Link*	*Link with Higher Tier/Fed*
Landless (33)	0.39	0.36	0.12	0.00	0.24	0.03
Small (274)	0.43	0.28	0.07	0.08	0.32	0.01
Large (43)	0.27	0.16	0.02	0.02	0.16	0.00
Overall (350)	0.41	0.28	0.07	0.07	0.30	0.01

Note: Figures in parentheses indicate the number of observations.

Table 7.5C: Effectiveness of Different Types of Extension Services on Group (SHG, PG, JLG) Formation with Respect to Extent of Local Level Familiarity of Sample Households

Extent of Familiarity of Households	*Effectiveness Indices (0–1) by Types of Extension Service in Allied Agriculture*					
	Formation of Self-Help Groups	*Creation of Norms of Behavior*	*Leadership Development*	*Knowledge of Book-Keeping*	*Help in SHG-Bank Link*	*Link with Higher Tier/Fed*
Nil (31)	0.35	0.35	0.06	0.00	0.03	0.00
Moderate (16)	0.31	0.12	0.06	0.00	0.18	0.00
High (303)	0.42	0.28	0.07	0.08	0.33	0.01
Overall (350)	0.41	0.28	0.07	0.07	0.30	0.01

Note: Figures in parentheses indicate the number of observations.

Table 7.5D: Effectiveness of Different Types of Extension Services on Group (SHG, PG, JLG) Formation with Respect to Educational Status of Sample Households

Educational Status of Households	*Effectiveness Indices (0–1) by Types of Extension Service in Allied Agriculture*					
	Formation of Self-Help Groups	*Creation of Norms of Behavior*	*Leadership Development*	*Knowledge of Book-Keeping*	*Help in SHG-Bank Link*	*Link with Higher Tier/Fed*
Illiterate (27)	0.51	0.51	0.14	0.11	0.37	0.00
Literate (96)	0.54	0.41	0.09	0..05	0.39	0.04
Educated (144)	0.38	0.22	0.05	0.06	0.29	0.01
Highly educated (83)	0.27	0.14	0.06	0.08	0.15	0.00

Note: Figures in parentheses indicate the number of observations.

Table 7.5E: Effectiveness of Different Types of Extension Services on Group (SHG, PG, JLG) Formation with Respect to Savings and Insurance Status of Sample Households

Savings and Insurance Status of Sample Households	*Effectiveness Indices (0–1) by Types of Extension Service in Allied Agriculture*					
	Formation of Self-Help Groups	*Creation of Norms of Behavior*	*Leadership Development*	*Knowledge of Book-Keeping*	*Help in SHG-Bank Link*	*Link with Higher Tier/Fed*
Nil (54)	0.46	0.20	0.03	0.03	0.27	0.01
Only savings (109)	0.58	0.44	0.11	0.10	0.37	0.02
Only insurance (25)	0.20	0.04	0.00	0.00	0.20	0.00
Both (162)	0.30	0.23	0.07	0.07	0.26	0.01

Note: Figures in parentheses indicate the number of observations.

in the three villages of Indian Sundarbans—namely, Choravidya, Dhuchnikhali and Khulna, where either an NGO or an NBFC is functioning. There is little bit of activities of group formation and norm-setting in the three villages of Bhatagaon, Kendri and Tarpongi, which seem to be in their infancy.

The indices of effectiveness of extension services related to borrower group formation seem to have a bias in favor of landless and small holding borrower households, which is expected (Table 7.5B). However, this bias is in favor of borrower households with strong degree of familiarity to locally important personnel (Table 7.5C). Table 7.5D displays some bias in favor of illiterate and just literate groups of borrowers, while Table 7.5E shows bias in favor of households having some savings.

7.7 EFFECTIVENESS OF GENERAL EXTENSION SERVICES AMONG BORROWERS

Although general extension services don't have always direct implications for individual credit, these services do have important connotations for boosting up credit demand as well as credit supply for creating collective facilities and making collective gains. Several extension activities are considered at this juncture e.g., creating general awareness, promoting cleanliness/sanitation, imparting knowledge on efficient fuel use, creating awareness about input use, value addition and output marketing, building up better customer relations, display of product/output, storage, repair/ maintenance works, contingent services and community improvement programs. The overall significance of these general extension services can

Table 7.6A: Effectiveness of General Types of Extension Services across Villages

	Effectiveness Indices (0–1) by Types of Extension Service in Allied Agriculture											
Village Name	*Awareness Camp*	*Cleanliness/ Sanitation*	*Efficient Fuel Use*	*Intelligence in Input Use*	*Knowledge of Value Addition*	*Marketing Intelligence*	*Promoting Customer Relation*	*Display of Output/Product*	*Knowledge of Storage/Rodents/Pest*	*Knowledge of Repair/Maintenance*	*Contingent Advisory Service*	*Community Improvement Program*
Bhatagaon (50)	0.42	0.22	0.10	0.00	0.02	0.00	0.00	0.00	0.14	0.04	0.00	0.06
Kendri (50)	0.88	0.08	0.20	0.04	0.08	0.02	0.00	0.24	0.30	0.18	0.00	0.06
Tarpongi (50)	0.82	0.00	0.00	0.00	0.02	0.02	0.00	0.02	0.42	0.14	0.00	0.00
Chorabidya (30)	0.96	0.96	0.23	0.03	0.00	0.00	0.00	0.00	0.00	0.03	0.00	0.00
Dhuchnikhali (30)	1.00	1.00	0.36	0.03	0.00	0.00	0.03	0.00	0.00	0.00	0.00	0.00
Khulna (50)	0.93	0.93	0.26	0.06	0.00	0.03	0.06	0.00	0.00	0.03	0.00	0.00
Madhusudankati (30)	0.80	0.86	0.83	0.63	0.33	0.33	0.20	0.33	0.26	0.00	0.03	0.00
Metiyakhali (30)	0.93	0.56	0.16	0.13	0.13	0.10	0.10	0.13	0.10	0.13	0.06	0.13
Kotha (50)	0.12	0.76	0.10	0.76	0.88	0.76	0.04	0.00	0.06	0.02	0.00	0.00

Note: Figures in parentheses represent number of observations.

Table 7.6B: Effectiveness of General Types of Extension Services with Respect to Operational Holding Status of Sample Households

	Effectiveness Indices (0–1) by Types of Extension Service in Allied Agriculture											
Operational Landholding Class	*Awareness Camp*	*Cleanliness/ Sanitation*	*Efficient Fuel Use*	*Intelligence in Input Use*	*Knowledge of Value Addition*	*Marketing Intelligence*	*Promoting Customer Relation*	*Display of Output/Product*	*Knowledge of Storage/Rodents/Pest*	*Knowledge of Repair/Maintenance*	*Contingent Advisory Service*	*Community Improvement Program*
Landless (33)	0.60	0.57	0.09	0.30	0.21	0.24	0.06	0.06	0.03	0.06	0.03	0.06
Small (274)	0.72	0.52	0.23	0.16	0.14	0.12	0.04	0.08	0.16	0.07	0.01	0.02
Large (43)	0.74	0.48	0.18	0.30	0.34	0.27	0.04	0.06	0.23	0.04	0.02	0.04
Overall (350)	0.71	0.52	0.21	0.19	0.18	0.15	0.04	0.07	0.16	0.07	0.01	0.02

Note: Figures in parentheses represent number of observations.

Table 7.6C: Effectiveness of General Types of Extension Services with Respect to Extent of Familiarity to Important Village/Local Personnel

Extent of Familiarity of Households	*Effectiveness Indices (0–1) by Types of Extension Service in Allied Agriculture*											
	Awareness Camp	*Cleanliness/ Sanitation*	*Efficient Fuel Use*	*Intelligence in Input Use*	*Knowledge of Value Addition*	*Marketing Intelligence*	*Promoting Customer Relation*	*Display of Output/Product*	*Knowledge of Storage/Rodents/Pest*	*Knowledge of Repair/Maintenance*	*Contingent Advisory Service*	*Community Improvement Program*
Nil (31)	0.41	0.22	0.09	0.00	0.00	0.00	0.00	0.00	0.19	0.06	0.00	0.06
Moderate (16)	0.50	0.06	0.12	0.06	0.00	0.06	0.12	0.00	0.12	0.12	0.00	0.00
High (303)	0.75	0.57	0.23	0.21	0.20	0.17	0.04	0.08	0.16	0.06	0.01	0.02
Overall (350)	0.71	0.52	0.21	0.19	0.18	0.15	0.04	0.07	0.16	0.07	0.01	0.02

Table 7.6D: Effectiveness of General Types of Extension Services with Respect to Maximum Male Educational Status of Sample Households

Maximum Male Education Status	*Effectiveness Indices (0–1) by Types of Extension Service in Allied Agriculture*											
	Awareness Camp	*Cleanliness/ Sanitation*	*Efficient Fuel Use*	*Intelligence in Input Use*	*Knowledge of Value Addition*	*Marketing Intelligence*	*Promoting Customer Relation*	*Display of Output/Product*	*Knowledge of Storage/Rodents/Pest*	*Knowledge of Repair/Maintenance*	*Contingent Advisory Service*	*Community Improvement Program*
Illiterate (27)	0.70	0.33	0.07	0.07	0.03	0.03	0.11	0.03	0.18	0.00	0.00	0.00
Literate (96)	0.81	0.55	0.23	0.06	0.03	0.04	0.01	0.05	0.15	0.05	0.02	0.04
Educated (144)	0.80	0.48	0.25	0.17	0.14	0.13	0.05	0.11	0.18	0.11	0.00	0.02
Highly educated (83)	0.48	0.61	0.18	0.40	0.45	0.36	0.03	0.04	0.12	0.04	0.00	0.02

be seen from the last row in Table 7.6C, where it is found that the effectiveness indices are pretty high in terms of organization of awareness camps and imparting knowledge on sanitation (being utilized by 71% and 52% sample borrowers, respectively), moderate for efficient fuel use, intelligence in input use, knowledge of value addition, marketing intelligence and knowledge of storage/rodents/pest (21%, 19%, 18%, 15% and 16%, respectively), but very low for others.

Table 7.6A gives the scores of different sample villages for different general extension services. The three villages of Chhatisgarh seem to have derived some benefits of general awareness creation, sanitation, and to a lesser extent, on storage, repair and maintenance, but in other components, their scores are close to zero. The three West Bengal villages from Indian Sunderbans display good scores for general awareness, sanitation, and to a lesser degree on fuel-efficient use, but their scores are nearly zero elsewhere. The two cooperatively stronger villages of West Bengal (i.e., Metiyakhali and Madhusudankati) have performed better also in fuel-use, input-use, value-addition, output marketing, customer relation, output display and storage. They continue to be weak in repair/ maintenance, contingency services and community improvement programs. The cooperatively strong village of Kotha from South Gujarat has done fairly well in sanitation, input use, value-addition and output marketing, but is found lagging in other dimensions of general extension services. So, even though existence of a well-functioning cooperative helps things, these co-operative are yet to undertake a lot of actions in several lagging dimensions.

As Table 7.6B shows, there is no strong association between the effectiveness indices of general extension services and land size holding of borrowers. Table 7.6C, however, shows some bias in favor of borrower households having strong familiarity to important local personnel. Table 7.6D shows bias slightly in favor of the last two groups of better educated borrowers only in respect of a few dimensions. The pattern of bias is somewhat stronger in favor of borrowers with insurance and both savings and insurance, in most of the dimensions.

7.8 SUMMARY AND CONCLUSION

Conceptually, one can think of the following roles of extension service in the context of rural credit. If good extension data are maintained over time not only on the extension inputs to the borrower's project, but also on the effectiveness of such inputs, these records can be utilized in future to separate out 'good' borrowers from 'bad' ones, thus resolving the adverse selection problem in credit. At the same time, a rigorous extension service coupled with monitoring can also put a check on opportunistic behavior of the borrower, besides saving the borrower's project under adverse contingent situations through supply of good advice and monitoring. By at least partially resolving the three above-stated problems of credit, it can boost up the lender's supply of credit, while in the longer run also boosting up demand from genuine borrowers. In fact, good extension service has the potential to improve performance of not only household credit, but also credit for collective/societal projects. For example, a good extension service on sanitation can not only create more awareness and thus boost up societal demand, but also, through creation of better extension-induced monitoring, provide an impetus to the society's willingness to meet the increased demand. These roles of extension services become all the more important in rural settings, which are often marred by market imperfections and market failures of various fronts.

The major findings on types and extent of extension service used in the context of credit are as follows:

- Within the sample, 90%, 71.4% and 13.7% borrowers are found to have user official extension services on agriculture, animal husbandry and fisheries, respectively. However, the moment we concentrate on borrowers incurring positive expenditure on extension services in these fields, the figures drop severely to 29.7%, 20.9% and 1.7%, respectively. Thus, we see that a large number of borrowers look up on extension as a free service i.e., they don't want to spend any money in procuring extension services nor in undertaking follow up actions, which will cost them money. This means that value of official extension services is too low in the minds of sample borrowers, given lack of awareness, on the one hand, and poor quality of government extension services, on the other. If we consider all relevant borrower groups, the indices of familiarity with government official extension services in these three fields are 0.85, 0.80 and 0.30 (against 0–3 scale) and their average annual expenditure on extension are found to be ₹ 677, ₹ 207 and ₹ 310 for groups practicing agriculture, animal husbandry and fishery, respectively. If we concentrate only on those borrowers who incur positive expenditure on extension, the familiarity indices shoot up to 1.7, 2 and 1, and average annual expenditure figures to ₹ 2055, ₹ 710 and ₹ 2050, respectively, for the same three groups.

- In respect of use of various sources of extension information, the sample borrowers are found to attach high importance to newspapers, neighbors/friends/relatives, television and radio (with utilization by proportions 0.72, 0.72, 0.61 and 0.60 of relevant borrowers, respectively). Opinion leaders/progressive farmers and farmer's club come next with utilization index of 0.28 each. The importance of extension bulletins and newsletter/magazines is moderately low (their indices being 0.15 and 0.18, respectively) whereas production guidelines and personal letters from extension agents have very little significance (with their importance index being 0.02 each). Obviously, there is immense room for improvement of extension education, especially through channels like production bulletin, neighbors, farmer's club, radio and television network.
- There are large variations in use of agricultural extension services across the sample villages. Thanks to the existence of an NGO called Youth Development center and an NBFC called Bandhan, the villages in Indian Sunderbans in West Bengal seem to have done pretty well in some aspects of agricultural extension. The villages of West Bengal and South Gujarat with well-known multipurpose PACS have also put up good performance in most dimensions of agricultural extension, but the picture in the three sample villages of Chhatisgarh remains much to be deserved.
- There is also high degree of variation in use of veterinary extension services across sample villages. While extension services on cattle/sheep/goat production, vaccination, health checkup, pregnancy check-up and external parasite spray are being used to some extent in all the villages, this is not true of other services like de-worming, artificial insemination, use of Azolla etc. and production of fishery, poultry, duckery and sericulture.
- As formation of peer group of borrowers is a critical instrument to make apparently credit-deprived borrowers credit-worthy, questions were asked to relevant borrowers about use of different types of extension services with respect to such groups. In cooperatively strong village of Kotha in Gujarat, SHGs are non-existent, though there seems to be ample room for SHG formation among landless households, to achieve an inclusive process of growth. However, in the two villages of West Bengal with relatively well-functioning cooperatives, these extension services seem to have made some dent. These extension services seem to have made a beginning also in the villages of Indian Sundarbans, where either an NGO or an NBFC is functioning. But these activities are only in their infancy in the three sample villages of Chhattisgarh.

- General extension services are hardly recognized as forces to boost up credit demand at both individual and collective levels. Nevertheless, their significance is found to be pretty high in terms of organization of awareness camps and imparting knowledge on sanitation (being utilized by 71% and 52% sample borrowers, respectively), moderate for efficient fuel use, intelligence in input use, knowledge of value addition, marketing intelligence and knowledge of storage/rodents/pest (21%, 19%, 18%, 15% and 16%, respectively).

Based on the above-stated findings, several conclusions now seem to be in order. First, it seems that the close linkage and possible interaction between credit and extension is neither fully appreciated, nor explored enough, except to some extent by informal lenders, some well-functioning multipurpose PACs, and some government/NABARD/ NGO-promoted or NBFC-promoted MFIs. Second, the quality of official extension services seems not good enough to arouse much enthusiasm among borrowers to take them seriously, or to incur sufficient expenditure either to procure extension knowledge, or to pursue it vigorously. Third, the close link between extension and monitoring, even when a few credit organizations (like Amalsad multipurpose PACS or BASIX) are found to be providing some beautiful examples, is often not formalized enough to get maximum value out of extension. For example, well-functioning multipurpose PACS may be informally using borrower response to their provision of extension services to gauge borrower's credibility, they have not formalized the same, nor do they have spent enough resources on extension. On the other hand, MFIs of both varieties seem to have, subject to their resource constraints, used extension more from a monitoring angle, rather than for imparting fresh knowledge to borrowers to augment the value of their projects. Fourth, general extension services, which too can augment both individual and collective body's effective demand for fresh credit, don't seem to be taken very seriously, except in some rare pockets and instances. As a result, whatever official or institutional extension services are there, seem to be far from complete or comprehensive to show up their impact on credit performance. Obviously, there is enormous room for action beyond the zone of complacence.

CHAPTER 8

Agricultural Debt Waiver and Debt Relief Scheme

8.1 INTRODUCTION

Considering the facts like low profitability in agriculture and high risk due to adverse climatic condition, asymmetric information, unnoticeable factors causing volatile price for agri-products, Government of India introduced a loan waiver scheme to get vulnerable farmers out of their indebtedness. In the Union Budget Speech, 2008–09, the then Finance Minister announced a Debt Waiver and Debt Relief scheme for farmers. It was stipulated that the scheme would cover agricultural loan reaching to small and marginal farmers through RRBs, Scheduled Commercial Bank (SCB) and Cooperative Credit Institutions. The number of beneficiaries was initially estimated at nearly 30 million small and marginal farmers and 10 million other farmers with an estimated cost of ₹ 60,000 crore. Later the beneficiaries turned out to be a figure of 37 million of small and marginal farmers and 5.97 million of other category farmers. The cost also increased to ₹ 71,680 crore[1].

In this chapter, a systematic attempt is made to assess how effective the scheme was to unlease the burden of the target group. It examines who benefited had from this scheme, and the nature of access to formal credit of the same beneficiaries in future, besides comparing characteristics of the beneficiaries vis-à-vis non-beneficiaries. In our sample, we have 350 households out of which 48 households are found to have enjoyed the benefit of loan waiver scheme.

This chapter is organized as follows. In the following section we provide an overview of the last debt waiver and debt relief scheme. The next

[1]The whys and hows of farm loan waiver scheme (24th May 2008). Business Standard.

section documents the research findings on how effective the scheme was to reach the target group. The last section concludes.

8.2 AN OVERVIEW OF THE SCHEME

The eligibility for debt waiver or debt relief, as the case may be, comprised of (a) in case of a short-term production loan, the amount of such loan (together with applicable interest), and (b) in the case of an investment loan, the installments of such loan that are overdue (together with applicable interest on such installments), if the loan was (i) disbursed up to March 31, 2007 and overdue as on December 31, 2007 and remaining unpaid until February 29, 2008; (ii) restructured and rescheduled by banks in 2004 and in 2006 through special packages announced by the Central Government, whether overdue or not; and (iii) restructured and rescheduled in the normal course up to March 31, 2007 as per applicable RBI guidelines on account of natural calamities, whether it became overdue or not.

The scheme implied full waiver of 'eligible amount' in case of small or marginal farmers, while it involved only, One Time Settlement (OTS) in case of 'other farmers', where the farmer would be given a rebate of 25 per cent of the 'eligible amount' subject to the condition that the farmer pays the balance of 75 per cent of the 'eligible amount'. In case of a farmer who had obtained investment credit for allied activities with the principal loan amount not exceeding ₹ 50,000, he would be classified as "small and marginal farmer" and, where the principal amount exceeded ₹ 50,000, he would be classified as 'other farmer', irrespective of the size of his land holding, in either case.

At the initial stage, the loan relief scheme was enthusiastically welcomed on the basis of government endeavor toward unleashing the accumulated debt of peasant communities. But later invited criticism on several grounds. Rath (2009)[2] in this regard argued that the debt waiver and debt relief scheme would adversely hurt the functioning of cooperatives by discouraging farmers to maintain good financial behavior. EPW Research Foundation (2008)[3] raised a pertinent question whether this scheme was conducive to sponsoring and strengthening a vigorous rural financial

[2] Rath, N. (2009). 'Implications of the Loan Waiver for Rural Credit Institutions', Economic and Political Weekly, 43 (24).

[3] EPW Research Foundation (2008). The Loan Waiver Scheme. Economic and Political Weekly, 43(11), 28–34.

structure, where asymmetric bargaining strength existed and also where bank executives are known to withdraw lending at the smallest signal of loan recoveries. Based on the assumption that small and marginal farmers are always out of the formal credit sources, Dev (2008)[4] felt that the scheme was not encouraging, and skewed towards irrigated and big farmers.

8.3 FINDINGS OF THE STUDY

In Table 8.1, borrowers are categorized in terms of their loan access as well as their household characteristics. Along the columns of this table, we are comparing the household characteristics of the recipients of loan waiver, non-recipients of the same scheme, and households with access to formal loan 2009–10, households with access to any loan in 2009–10, and all 350-sample households. The several household characteristic being examined across rows are: caste and religion, poverty status, farmer type, education status, farm implement holding status, household asset holding status and familiarity with locally important personnel (in panels A to G, respectively). Percentages of row totals are indicated in brackets in each cell. A comparison of these percentage figures across columns thus indicate whether or not the recipients of loan waiver have distinctive characteristics in terms of this attributes, as compared to the other borrower groups displayed in other columns of this table. Although SC/ST/OBC categories are dominant among recipients of loan waiver (about 65 %), scheme of 2007–08, there seems to be some upper caste buyers among these beneficiaries. In terms of poverty status, BPL categories are more dominant (about 58 %), and there is also a biased in favor of this category among beneficiaries. Among size groups of farmers, small farmers are most dominant (about 92 %); there is also a biased in favor of this group among recipients of loan waiver. In terms of educational status, the recipients of loan waiver are fairly well spread among different educational classes, though there seems to be a slight biased against highly educated categories. Among farm implement holding status of loan waiver beneficiaries, households holding no implements are the most dominant (about 56 %), but it is moderately equipped households which seem to have enjoyed some edge among loan waiver beneficiaries. Within different household asset holding groups, those without any household asset seem to have been under-represented and

[4] Dev, S.M. (2008). Agriculture: Absence of a Big Push. Economic and Political Weekly, 43(15), 33–39.

those with moderate asset holding seem to have been over-represented. In terms of familiarity with important local level personnel, it is the group with moderate familiarity with locally important personnel, which has enjoyed some favor among loan waiver beneficiaries, though the most dominant category (about 85%) is among borrowers with good local level familiarity. Thus, in terms of various observable borrower characteristics, one can say that although borrowers in BPL categories, small land holding groups moderately equipped households in terms of farm implements and household assets, and also those with moderate degree of familiarity with locally important personnel have enjoyed better representation among loan waiver beneficiaries, it is also true that there is some bias in favor of upper caste households.

Table 8.1: Distinctive Characteristics of Borrowers Benefited from Loan Waiver Scheme

Household Characteristics	*Recipients of Loan Waiver (Total 48)*	*Non-Recipients of Loan Waiver (Total 200)*	*Households with Access to Formal Loan in 2009–10 (Total 208)*	*Households with Access to any Loan in 2009–10 (Total 302)*	*All Sample Households (Total 350)*
A. Caste and Religion					
1. Upper Caste	16 (33.33)	63 (31.50)	60 (28.85)	84 (27.81)	97 (27.71)
2. SC/ST/OBC	31 (64.58)	127 (63.50)	144 (69.23)	203 (67.22)	237 (67.71)
3. Religious minority	1 (2.08)	10 (5.00)	4 (1.92)	15 (4.97)	16 (4.51)
B. Poverty Status					
1. BPL	28 (58.33)	99 (49.50)	106 (50.96)	165 (54.64)	184 (52.57)
2. APL	20 (41.67)	101 (50.50)	102 (49.04)	137 (45.36)	166 (47.43)
C. Farmer Size Groups					
1. Landless	1 (2.08)	17 (8.50)	10 (4.81)	25 (9.28)	33 (9.43)
2. Small	44 (91.67)	151 (75.50)	162 (77.88)	235 (77.81)	274 (78.29)
3. Large	3 (6.25)	32 (16.00)	36 (17.31)	42 (13.91)	43 (12.29)

Table contd...

Table 8.1 contd...

Household Characteristics	*Recipients of Loan Waiver (Total 48)*	*Non-Recipients of Loan Waiver (Total 200)*	*Households with Access to Formal Loan in 2009–10 (Total 208)*	*Households with Access to any Loan in 2009–10 (Total 302)*	*All Sample Households (Total 350)*
D. Education Status					
1. Illiterate	3 (6.25)	12 (6.00)	8 (3.85)	19 (6.29)	27 (7.71)
2. Literate	13 (27.08)	50 (25.00)	42 (20.19)	81 (26.82)	96 (27.43)
3. Educated	22 (45.83)	91 (45.50)	100 (48.08)	135 (44.70)	144 (41.14)
4. Highly Educated	10 (20.83)	47 (23.50)	58 (27.88)	67 (22.19)	83 (23.71)
E. Farm Implement Holding Status					
1. Nil	27 (56.25)	112 (56.00)	113 (54.33)	174 (57.62)	198 (56.57)
2. Moderately Equipped	13 (27.08)	38 (19.00)	44 (21.15)	60 (19.87)	73 (20.86)
3. Well Equipped	8 (16.67)	50 (25.00)	51 (24.52)	68 (22.52)	79 (22.57)
F. Household Asset Holding Status					
1. Nil	2 (4.17)	16 (8.00)	15 (7.21)	24 (7.95)	26 (7.43)
2. Less	11 (22.92)	50 (25.00)	47 (22.60)	87 (28.81)	90 (25.71)
3. Moderate	27 (56.25)	79 (39.50)	85 (40.87)	118 (39.07)	147 (42.00)
4. Good	8 (16.67)	55 (27.50)	61 (29.33)	73 (24.17)	87 (24.86)
G. Familiarity with Locally Important Personnel					
1. Nil	2 (4.17)	8 (4.00)	4 (1.92)	16 (5.30)	31 (8.86)
2. Moderate	5 (10.42)	8 (4.00)	8 (3.85)	13 (4.30)	16 (4.57)
3. Good	41 (85.42)	184 (92.00)	196 (94.23)	273 (90.40)	303 (86.57)

Note: Figure in parentheses is column percentages under every section of characteristics.

Table 8.2 provides a frequency distribution of 2007–08 loan waiver beneficiary scheme across loan sources, besides their access to credit from the same formal sources during 2008–09. It is see that only 48 out of 350 sample borrowers got the benefit of this scheme during 2007–08, but only 50 % of them could access formal loan sources during 2008–09. Obviously this does not speak highly about the loan waiver scheme as providing better access to the same sources in future. During 2007–08, about 71 % of loan waiver beneficiaries were from PACS/multipurpose PACS, while only 21 % and 8 % of the beneficiaries were associated with RRBs and commercial banks, respectively. By 2008–09 (i.e., by the next year) the access of the beneficiary group to loans from commercial banks and RRB dropped to 4.17 % and 0 % shares, respectively. Although the shares of PACS and multipurpose PACS have increased from 71 % to 86 %, only 23 among 34 beneficiaries could access loan during 2008–09. It seems that while the loan waiver scheme has temporarily benefited some small number of households in the short-run, the fact that these beneficiaries were really defaulters of loan made them severely susceptible to loan refusal in the next year. In other words, the loan waiver scheme not only discouraged good borrower behavior but also severely penalized the beneficiary group in terms of their future loan access to the same formal sources. For commercial banks and RRBs, the percentage shares of loan waiver beneficiaries dropped drastically to 4 % and 0 %, respectively.

Table 8.2: Frequency of Distribution of Loan Waiver Beneficiaries across Different Sources of Formal Credit during 2007–08 and 2008–09

Sources of Credit	*2007–08*	*2008–09*
Commercial Bank	4 (8.33)	1 (4.17)
RRB	10 (20.83)	0
PACS	29 (60.42)	19 (79.17)
Multi Purpose PACS	5 (10.42)	4 (16.67)
Sub-Total	**48**	**24**

Table 8.3 shows some borrowers' side information emanating from their experience involved in availing benefit of loan relief scheme. Accumulated debts of each category of farmers are more or less same. It is interesting to note that small farmers have repaid a part of their principal amount of loan, thus their accumulated debt amount stands around 67 per cent of

the loan amount. Large farmers, on the other hand, are found to be facing a debt burden as high as 97 per cent of the borrowed amount. Large farmers are thus able to derive the maximum benefit, around 99 per cent of the accumulated debt, while for small farmers the same figure turns out to be 93 per cent. Further number of trips to avail the benefit is more in case of small farmers as compared to the same for large farmers. Small farmers also seem to have faced higher transaction cost as compared to large farmers to avail the benefit. For small farmers, the transaction cost is more than four per cent of the total benefit amount, while the same for large farmers is around one percent of total benefit. The extent of gap between announcement and disbursement of benefits of the scheme is fairly uniform across land holding groups.

Table 8.3: Borrower Side Information on Loan Waiver Scheme across Land Holding Groups

Land	*Accumulated Debt up to March 31, 2007*	*Principal Loan Amount*	*Interest Charged*	*Number of Trips Made to Avail the Benefits*	*Amount Benefit*	*Benefit as % of Debt*	*Expenditure to Avail the Benefit (in ₹)*	*Expenditure as % of Benefit*	*Gap between Announcement and Disbursement of Benefit Amount in Months*
Landless (1)	8000	8000	7%	2	8000	100.0	350.0	4.4	2
Small farmer (44)	7245.59	10702.94	8.12%	2.7	6798.5	93.8	281.7	4.1	1.7
Large farmer (3)	7166.67	7333.33	9.7%	1.3	7116.5	99.3	88.3	1.2	2

Table 8.4 examines whether those who had access to formal sources in 2007–08 (both loan waiver beneficiaries and non-beneficiaries) are still having access to formal channel in 2009–10. More specifically this table tries to examine whether the hierarchical structure observed among borrowers during 2007–08 got altered or not as a result of the loan waiver scheme. The rows of this table have arranged the borrowers in a hierarchical structure starting from those who did not get any loan during 2007–08 at the bottom with borrowers having exclusively informal sector access in the next higher layer, borrowers with access to formal loan and without or with benefit of loan waiver in the next higher up scales, while those who did not apply for loans during 2007–08 are put at the top of the hierarchical system. Among the borrowers in 2009–10, we could demarcate those with formal sector access from those having access exclusively to informal sector and those without any access at all. If we go along the percentage figures in rows, we can see

that among the 15 households who did not get any loan in 2007–08, only 1 could access the formal sector, another 6 to the exclusively informal sector, and as many as 8 remained without access to any source. Among 41 households having access exclusively to informal source in 2007–08, only 17% could access formal loan in the next year while 54% and 29% remained dependent on exclusively informal sector and no source, respectively during the next year. Among 200 borrowers having access to formal source but without loan waiver benefits in 2007–08, 69% continued to maintain their formal sector access during the next year, while 22% and 9% of them were relegated to exclusively informal source and no access categories, respectively during the next year. Among borrowers having access to formal source with benefits of loan waiver, 15% and 8% got pushed to exclusively informal and no access sources, respectively. Among 46 borrowers in 2007–08, who did not apply for loan during the earlier period, only 57% could access formal source during the next year. Thus, we see that there is no significant change in the hierarchy of loan access between 2007–08 and 2008–09, as reflected in the value of chi-square in this table.

Table 8.4: Interaction between Deferent Patterns of Loan Access in 2007–08 and 2009–10 Scenario

2007–08 Status of the Borrowers in Terms of their Loan Holding	*2009–10 Status of the Borrowers in Terms of their Loan Holding*			
	Formal Access	*Exclusively Informal*	*No Access*	*Sub-Total*
Did Not Apply for Loan	26 (57)	14 (30)	6 (13)	46
Formal Loan Holder with Loan waiver	37 (77)	7 (15)	4 (8)	48
Formal Loan Holder without Loan Waiver	137 (69)	45 (22)	18 (9)	200
Exclusively Informal	7 (17)	22 (54)	12 (29)	41
Did Not Get any Loan	1 (7)	6 (40)	8 (53)	15
Sub Total	208 (59)	94 (27)	48 (14)	**350**

Statistic	*DF*	*Value*	*Prob*
Chi-Square	**8**	**69.6818**	**< .0001**
Likelihood Ratio Chi-Square	8	68.1541	< .0001
Contingency Coefficient		**0.4075**	

Note: Figure in parentheses indicates row percentages.

8.4 SUMMARY AND CONCLUSION

Although loan waiver and debt relief schemes are usually politically oriented, from the view point of liberal economic thinking we have examined in this chapter (i) whether the scheme was targeted well in favor of socio-economically weaker groups, (ii) whether one time benefit of loan waiver or debt relief could promote continuous access of the beneficiary groups to the formal sources, and (iii) whether this scheme could favorably alter the hierarchy among borrowers between 2007–08 and 2008–09. Our findings in this chapter indicate that although the benefit was largely captured by borrowers with socio-economic status, it was mostly because of their predominance in the sample. In fact, there are indications that this scheme favored large farmers as well as those with moderate level of affluence, as reflected in their characteristics. The scheme clearly failed to augment or even maintain formal sector access of the beneficiaries, not to speak of altering the hierarchy among different types of borrowers from low end without any access to the high end with access deliberately not used.

CHAPTER 9

Summary, Conclusion and Recommendations

9.1 BACKGROUND

Scarcity of credit not only to meet working capital gap and investment needs, but also to meet consumption shortfalls in lean period or contingent situations, of rural households has long been recognized by policy makers. Since British colonial period, India has therefore witnessed several government interventions to extend the reach of formal banking service. A Land Mortgage Bank was established in late 19th century. Cooperative Credit Societies Act came in 1904. After Independence, major move in this direction was nationalization of 14 commercial banks in 1969, with addition of six more banks under state ownership in 1980. Stipulation of disbursement targets to agriculture, small scale and cottage industries (priority sector) started in 1975. Regional Rural Bank (RRB) was set up in the same year to augment rural lending. In 1977, Reserve Bank of India (RBI) came out with 1:4 branch licensing policy, which stipulated that to open one branch in a banked area, the bank would have to open four branches in a non-banked area. In 1982, the National Bank for Agriculture and Rural Development (NABARD) was established as an apex development institution. The government also announced repeated debt forgiveness schemes on account of periodic, but widespread inability of farmers to repay loans, the latest one being in 2008. By end of the last decade, government made short-term credit available at six per cent annual rate of interest. Such policy interventions are all intended to boost up private investment in agriculture.

A close scrutiny of published documents indicates that even after a century of systematic effort and establishment of wide network of delivery channel, the reach of banking service is not satisfactory and there lies several weaknesses in the rural credit delivery mechanism, such as high transaction cost, bankers' inclination towards collateral based financing, minimalist credit approach etc. to name a few. On the other hand, government surveys highlight that informal agencies provided 42.3 per cent of the outstanding loans of rural households in 2002 as against 30.6 per cent in 1991–92, a considerable increase in their market share. This outcome became a matter of serious concern, as government policy always intended to reach the excluded with subsidized credit, while most state governments took pro-active steps to restrict the operation of private moneylenders.

9.2 OBJECTIVES OF THE STUDY

Given this backdrop, the present study is undertaken with the following objectives: (i) to assess whether all segments of Indian rural economy interested in credit (including allied agricultural activities) are really getting access to credit; (ii) whether credit is being efficiently delivered to them in right quantity and quality; and (iii) at appropriate terms and conditions, which they can afford. The study is undertaken keeping in mind the government policy of cheap and concessional credit including recent debt waiver and debt relieve scheme, on the one hand, and emergence of 'credit plus' approach—a multi-market intervention followed by various new generation MFIs as well as multipurpose cooperative societies to address the multifarious problems involved in delivery of rural credit, on the other hand. Thus, it is also intended to examine whether available credit is being complemented by necessary extension services either from government extension agencies or, directly from credit agencies, to contribute towards livelihood promotion of borrowers and sustainable development of both borrowers and lenders.

9.3 CONCEPTUAL FRAMEWORK

As credit involves exchange of future endowments with current resources, it necessitates trust between the two negotiating parties to lock a deal. Given high information asymmetry between lender and his prospective borrowers, lenders usually ask for marketable collateral to bridge the gap in mutual trust (if any). Commercial banks inclusive of RRBs, due to high transaction cost involved in gathering information as well as monitoring the action of a large number of scattered borrowers, heavily rely on collateral backed project financing. This keeps resource scarce sections of rural community, who are in dearth of collateral acceptable to formal financial channel but in pressing need of financing their consumption needs, outside the domain of formal financial channel. Since the market for credit is very much prone to the problems of market failure due to adverse selection (of both borrower and lender), moral hazard (i.e. willful or induced default) and hold up problem (i.e. non-willful default due to multiple risks beyond control of either the borrower or the lender), it is pertinent to examine whether and to what extent the process of credit delivery and credit repayment conforms to the safeguards against the various reasons for market failure, and whether government regulation and interventions have helped overcome these problems.

'Efficiency' of credit delivery mechanism means not only availability of credit in right quantity, but also its availability in right quality i.e., available at the right time and with minimum response time depending upon the loan purpose. Credit must also be available to the borrower at appropriate terms and conditions, which he can afford. Terms and conditions of credit cover a whole spectrum of price and price like parameters such as interest rate, the mode of interest charging, repayment schedule, borrowers' transaction cost, borrowers' collateral demanded, flexibility in repayment of credit etc. In fact, the terms and conditions of credit must also cover the lenders' cost of credit including various risks confronted and subsumed by the lender. No organization of credit can survive unless it earns at least a normal rate of profit from its credit operations.

On the issue of equitable distribution of the benefits of credit, the pertinent question is whether the gains of credit, i.e., borrower's surplus and lender's surplus (in the language of market economics) are fairly distributed between the two sides. Similarly a sustainable credit system needs to be commercially viable in the long run, for both the sides of a loan.

9.4 STUDY METHODOLOGY, SAMPLING DESIGN AND COVERAGE

Against the above stated theoretical issues, the study aims to analyze available borrower and lender side information under alternative credit scenarios, as elaborated below:

Step 1: The study is undertaken in two states—namely, Chhattisgarh and West Bengal. Given rather low order of penetration of MFIs in the country or a state as a whole, but presence of clusters of such organizations, a cluster of MFIs is chosen from each of these states in the first place, before selecting 3–5 villages from that cluster such that all forms of credit organizations—formal, semiformal and informal are functioning in those villages taken together to test implications of contestability across various lending organizations. Formal sources are again categorized into two—formal 1, which includes scheduled government or private commercial banks and RRBs, and formal 2 including all types of cooperative banks—namely, PACS, multi-purpose PACS and their higher-tier bodies. Similarly, semi-formal source has two components, the first referring to MFIs promoted by government/NABARD/NGOs, whereas the second refers to only those MFIs, which are promoted by private NBFCs. Informal sources of credit are divided into two categories—the first includes only traditional moneylenders, as commonly understood, whereas the second includes all other informal lenders like friends, relatives, traders, merchants, grocery shopkeepers, medical shops etc.

Step 2: Once a cluster of 3–5 villages within a single agro-climatic region of a state is selected, the next step is to canvass three different types of questionnaires for these villages: (i) a village questionnaire to identify and record village level demographic, land use, infrastructure, and government (schematic) intervention parameters, which may have an impact on credit delivery and credit use; (ii) lender-level questionnaire to seek some broad information from 2–3 major lending organizations within each selected village on their business and experience on loan waiver/relief; and (iii) a questionnaire to perform complete enumeration of all village households[1] on the basis of some of their credit experiences both before March 2007 (the cut-off date for loan waiver/relief scheme) and after March 2008 (the announcement date for the above-mentioned scheme), so that a suitable stratified sample of borrower households together with suitable controls can be drawn for the last stage of data collection.

Step 3: Assuming a total of five villages from each state, from each village 20 sample farmer households from agriculture and allied activities, and another five from non-farm sector are drawn on the basis of probability proportionate stratified random sampling. Two criteria are judiciously used for purpose of stratification: (i) source of borrowing—broadly, whether formal or non-formal; and (ii) the landholding class of the borrower—whether landless, small or large. Obviously, within the category of formal sector borrowers, we shall encounter households benefiting or not benefiting from loan waiver/relief scheme. At the same time, another control of five households per village are drawn using stratified random sampling principle to represent households, who didn't apply for loan or didn't get a loan prior to March 2007 (though they had asked for). So, assuming a total sample of 30 households from each village and

[1] If a village is too large in terms of number of households, some representative hamlets of that village (not exceeding 300 households) are used for complete enumeration. In that case, only those households covered under complete enumeration constitute the population from which the sample (both treatment and control) is drawn.

5 villages from each state, there would be 30 × 5 = 150 households per state[2]. Only one village of Gujarat under a famous multipurpose PACS, known for its strong credit-plus orientation, is chosen as another control. Each of the sample households is canvassed two questionnaires—one to solicit general information about household parameters, and the other to solicit only credit-related information like their access to various sources of credit, experienced terms and conditions of credit and their overall experiences with loan waiver/relief, credit delivery, interlinked credit transactions and credit-plus services. Thus, the total size of the sample for this study turns out to be 350 borrower households[3]. The section below summarizes the major findings of the study.

9.5 STUDY FINDINGS

On the issue of access to credit, the rural households are asked first, which sources they can potentially access for credit, given their past experiences, and second, which sources they have actually accessed for credit during 2009–10. The former is referred to as potential access, whereas the latter is as actual access. The main findings in this context are as follows:

- The cooperative banking sector, wherever it exists and is functioning fairly well, has the capacity to raise a decent expectation in the minds of borrowers as a highly potential source of credit. It has also the capacity to convert potential into actual supply of credit generally far better than the other sources. Further, it is found to have provided multiple loans to borrowers on several occasions.
- The commercial banking sector inclusive of RRBs has generally played a marginal role, very rarely exceeding 10.0% coverage in terms of catering to the demands of actual loanees. True, this source has also extended multiple loans per loanee, but their capacity to convert borrowers' expectations (as a potential source) into actual supply of loan is rather meager.
- The fact that the importance of traditional moneylenders in terms of providing access is about 14% on average in the total sample, and that sometimes it is as high as 24%, indicates the level of dependence

[2] In West Bengal, 5 villages with samples of 30 households each are taken to cover all types of lending institutions, whereas in Chhattisgarh, 3 villages are found enough to cover all types of lending organizations. So, a sample of 50 borrowers from each of the 3 villages of Chhattisgarh are picked up to match the sample size from West Bengal.

[3] This study is based on only borrower side information as detailed lender side information are not available except for some broad and general ones.

by rural households on this source, on the one hand, and also for the failure of our formal credit delivery mechanism, on the other.

- The most spectacular source of credit is informal channel covering a host of local lenders—friends, relatives, contractual parties, local shopkeepers, etc. This segment of lenders can provide easy access, not only by providing assurance as a potential supplier, but also through easily converting such assurances into realities. This source has also extended multiple loans per borrower.
- Well functioning cooperatives as well as newly evolved semiformal sectors (i.e., MFIs promoted by Government/NABARD/NGO or NBFCs) seem to have restricted the penetration of the informal source to some extent and found to be providing good competition, especially to the traditional informal lenders.

However, for credit to become a catalyst for livelihood promotion, it needs to be available to the borrower at terms and conditions, which he can afford. The major findings on terms and conditions experienced by the sample borrowers are as follows:

- The study finds that out of 574 loan cases among 350 sample households during 2009–10, only 43 loans are availed from formal commercial banking sector and RRBs, 193 from cooperative sector, 53 from SHGs promoted by government/NABARD/NGOs, whereas NBFC-promoted MFIs generate only 22 loan cases. The traditional rural moneylenders provide 54 loans, whereas the largest number of loan cases (209) are generated by the other rural lending agencies like friends, relatives, traders, merchants, shopkeepers etc.
- Commercial banks cum RRBs have provided the largest loan amount (nearly ₹ 80,000) on average, followed by cooperatives (more than ₹ 27,000), NBFC-promoted MFIs (slightly more than ₹ 11,000), local moneylenders (₹ 7,500), and other informal lenders (₹ 8,500) whereas government/NABARD/NGO-promoted MFIs provide the lowest-sized loan (₹ 4,700). So, it is natural to believe that for large loans, there is hardly any substitute for the commercial banking source.
- Only a few sources (e.g., supplying inputs, groceries, medicines etc., or marketing of produce) not only because of their proximity and closeness to borrower, but also sometimes because of the nature of their own activities, are found to be in a position to provide part of the loan in kind, taking advantage of complementarities between credit and a few pertinent services the borrower needs for effective use of credit.

- Though interest rates can't be compared unless and until the borrower's loan cycle is kept in mind, based on comparable annualized rates, interest rate charged is found to be the highest for traditional moneylenders (60 %), as expected.
- Regarding the modes of interest rate collection, as many as 20 % have zero interest rate, 31.83 % have interest charged on flat basis, and 48.17 % cases have interest charged on diminishing balance. Further, the incidence of upfront collection of interest is found to be highest among the private MFIs.
- Loans are found to be taken for three main purposes—as input in production (47.04 % of cases), to support consumption (43.38 %), and also for human capital investment (for example, for education, medical treatment and marriages), the incidence of the last category being only 9.58 %.
- Among the sample loan cases, as much as 49.13 % have no security or collateral. Almost 95 % of the loans produced by local lenders (informal-2) belong to this category, as these types of lenders, because of their proximity to and intimate knowledge of the borrowers, are in a position to provide loans without collateral. Next to trust, the second most important type of collateral used is mortgaging of farmland (21.60 %). The formal credit sources and traditional moneylenders have a strong liking for this type of collateral.
- In terms of overall flexibility in loan repayment, certain sources like cooperatives and the two types of informal lenders seem to have displayed more flexibility as compared to the commercial banking sector and the two semi-formal sources.
- Contrary to common belief, default rate is moderately high for the two informal sources—(11.11 % and 4.78 %, respectively, in terms of loans cases, and 6.32 % and 6.69 %, respectively, in terms of loan amount). For the two informal sources, percentage of loan amount overdue is smaller (10.81 % and 6.27 %, respectively), as compared to percentage of loan overdue cases (28 % and 22.28 %, respectively). SHG groups promoted by government/NABARD/NGOs has only 1.89 % of loan overdue cases and 2.08 % of loan amount overdue, thus displaying best performance against defaults. In contrast, NBFC-promoted MFIs have 9.09 % and 4.09 % overdue in terms of loan cases and loan amounts, respectively.
- Given the high degree of complementarily across sources it would be unwise to push further the agenda to get rid of informal and semi-formal sources. While the SCBs/RRBs seem to have comparative advantages in producing larger size loans with little credit plus

services, cooperatives, given their vast network and long standing experience, seem to have comparative advantages in producing small to medium size loans. Through sufficient cooperative sector reforms, this village level institution along with government/NABARD/NGO-promoted SHGs may be a viable vehicle to pass on the benefits of various government schemes at minimum transaction cost from both the sides. NBFC-promoted MFIs may be encouraged to be more transparent, competitive and accountable from the viewpoints of borrowers and entrusted with the job of filling the void between formal and informal sector credit. When credit plus services must go as a package to small borrowers, there are sufficient reasons to support complementarily among credit sources.

In the process of accessing loan from any source, a borrower incurs several types of transaction costs, which can be looked upon as an excess burden on the borrower beyond what he pays to the lender in terms of repayment of the principal with interest. Some of these costs are explicit and some are implicit, and only a few can be expressed in monetary terms to arrive at an overall estimate of borrower transaction cost. Many of the transaction costs, which are rather unobservable, remain outside the orbit of any estimation or analysis. In these circumstances, the present study has attempted to estimate only two types of borrower transaction costs as elaborated below:

- First, the transaction cost which the borrower incurs in terms waiting for sanction and disbursal of loans, commercial banking sector cum RRBs has the worst record of 23.71 days. Cooperative banks come next, involving 12.95 days of waiting on average. Loans from NBFCs involve 10.22 days of waiting, while the traditional rural moneylender takes about 7.86 days to sanction and disburse a loan. SHGs promoted by government/NABARD/NGOs take exactly 7 days, while the other informal rural moneylenders like friends, relatives, traders, merchants, shopkeepers, etc. take the minimum amount of time—precisely 4.41 days, to release a loan.
- In terms of monetary transaction cost the borrower incurs in searching for alternatives, approaching the final lender through several trips to him and paying to him in the form of application fees, documentation fees and processing fees, the general presumption is that the informal and semi-formal lenders must be having a strong comparative advantage relative to the formal lending organizations. This presumption is belied by the findings of this study, when the borrower transaction costs are expressed as percentage of the loan amount, in

view of the fact that much larger size loan is provided by commercial banks cum RRBs and cooperative banks (about ₹ 80,000 and 28,000, respectively) as compared to the loan size of other lenders (varying between ₹ 4.7 thousand to ₹ 11.2 thousand). Thus, borrower transaction costs turn out to be much less in percentage terms for the first two categories of formal sector lenders (namely, 1.91% and 1.43%, respectively) as compared to the two semi-formal sources (6.01% and 7.28%, respectively) and the two informal sources (6.32% and 0.08%, respectively).

In the process of availing a loan, a borrower may choose between interlinked and non-interlinked transactions. In case of interlinked transaction, the terms of trade in the services provided are simultaneously determined. While majority of lenders from formal sector credit follow a minimalist credit approach (i.e., providing credit alone), a few new generation semi-formal institutions (e.g., NBFC-promoted MFIs) as well as multipurpose cooperative societies are offering credit as well as complementary services—in the spirit of a multimarket intervention, popularly known as 'credit plus' approach. The present study has attempted to identify the context, nature and extent of interlinked transactions across lenders and up to what extent 'credit plus' approach is successful in filling in the lacuna (if any) left out by its minimalist counterpart. The main findings in this regard are:

- In the context of interlinked credit, availability of right quality of input, adverse climatic condition and natural catastrophe are reported to be the most important problems faced by borrowers while utilizing production loans.
- In most cases, borrowers are found to be resorting to individual efforts in addressing various problems in production, followed by help from 'credit plus' provider and support from neighbor, as the next two reports.
- It is observed that in the three villages under Indian Sunderbans in West Bengal, the borrowers have reported maximum problem in using production loan, as these villages are mostly under 'minimalist credit' approach, though they are enjoying some extension services from a local NGO or an NBFC-promoted MFI. On the other hand the two villages which have handled most of the problems satisfactorily (namely, Madhusudankathi of West Bengal and Kotha of Gujarat) are under the service area of strong 'Credit Plus' providers.
- Input-credit, output-credit and consumable-credit are found as the most important types of interlinked credit transactions in the study.

While the former two are mostly found under multipurpose PACS, consumable-credit interlinking is found to be a common feature in case of loans from local traders like cloth merchants, grocery/medical shopkeepers etc.

- Through both input-credit and output-credit arrangements, the farmers are found to have realized on average around three per cent price benefit. On the contrary, consumable-credit interlinking, which is mostly in private domain, has turned out to be on average 11.24 per cent costlier over non-linked cash transactions.

In the context of credit use, good extension services are observed to have the potential to improve performance of not only household credit, but also credit for collective/societal projects. If good extension data are maintained over time not only on the extension inputs to the borrower's project, but also on the effectiveness of such inputs, these records can be utilized in future to separate out 'good' borrowers from 'bad' ones, thus resolving the adverse selection problem in credit. At the same time, a rigorous extension service coupled with monitoring can also put a check on opportunistic behavior of the borrower, besides saving the borrower's project under adverse contingent situations through supply of good advice and monitoring. The empirical results in this context are:

- Within the sample, 90%, 71.4% and 13.7% borrowers are found to have used official extension services on agriculture, animal husbandry and fisheries, respectively. A meager proportion availing fisheries extension is primarily due to fisheries as an employment generating activity is limited in the sample.
- In respect of use of various sources of extension information, the sample borrowers are found to attach high importance to newspapers, neighbors/friends/relatives, television and radio.
- There are large variations in use of extension services across the sample villages. With the existence of an NGO called Youth Development center and an NBFC called Bandhan, the villages in Indian Sundarbans in West Bengal seem to have done pretty well in some aspects of agricultural extension. The villages of West Bengal and South Gujarat with well-known multipurpose PACS have also put up good performance in most dimensions of agricultural extension, but the picture in the three sample villages of Chhattisgarh remains much to be deserved.

As part of its objectives, the study has also aimed to identify (i) whether the loan waiver/relief scheme is targeted well in favor of socio-economically weaker groups, (ii) whether one time benefit of loan waiver or debt relief could promote continuous access of the beneficiary groups to the formal sources, and (iii) whether this scheme could favorably alter the hierarchy among borrowers between 2007–08 and 2008–09. A close scrutiny of the data from this study indicates that although the benefit is largely captured by borrowers from lower socio-economic status, it is mostly because of their predominance in the sample. In fact, there are indications that this scheme has favored large farmers as well as those with moderate level of affluence. The scheme has failed to augment or even maintain formal sector access of the beneficiaries, not to speak of altering the hierarchy among different types of borrowers from low end without any access to the high end where affluent borrowers have the liberty of not using their access to formal sources.

9.6 MAJOR CONCLUSIONS

Almost continuous and consistent failure of commercial banking sector cum RRBs to meet priority sector lending seems to be flowing from certain myths about credit, which has been persistently harbored by policy making circles for a long time. These myths arise primarily from two fundamental misconceptions—first, that credit is just like transaction in any other commodity/product like, say, apples, where spot market transactions are feasible, and are in fact the order of the day, and second, that credit risk can almost invariably be hedged by incorporating a marketable collateral and a credit-worthy project in the eyes of the banker to ensure safe loan repayment. However, facts are quite different. First of all, credit invariably involves a transaction between two parties over two points in time, during which many lapses can occur. So, credit cannot stand-alone; it must be backed by an act of trust on the part of the borrower. This means, supplying credit at a price below market clearing level (i.e., supplying cheap credit), although it offers some opportunity to the lender to screen out doubtful borrowers (i.e., avoiding adverse selection problem), does not resolve the two post-contractual problems of 'opportunism' on the part of the borrower and possible 'holdup problem' (i.e., locking-in effect) in the presence of unforeseen contingencies beyond the control of the borrower. Therefore, to solve the problems of credit market failure, the creditor must evolve dynamic systems and processes to control problems of willful and non-willful default from the side of the borrower. This is precisely what an informal lender does through spending his valuable time and resources. So, a credit, to be sustainable, has to be considered in a dynamic general equilibrium format, rather than in a 'credit alone' (i.e., a 'minimalist credit' approach in todays' parlance) partial equilibrium framework. Very often the creditor following a static partial equilibrium approach and offering credit at concessional rates (see, Figure 9.1 below) tends to forget that his approach will invariably produce a deadweight loss triangle, implying efficiency loss, which a smart lender (as well as sensible borrower) will try to avoid through instituting various terms and conditions, besides involving several credit-complementary services to ensure optimality in a suitable multi-market framework.

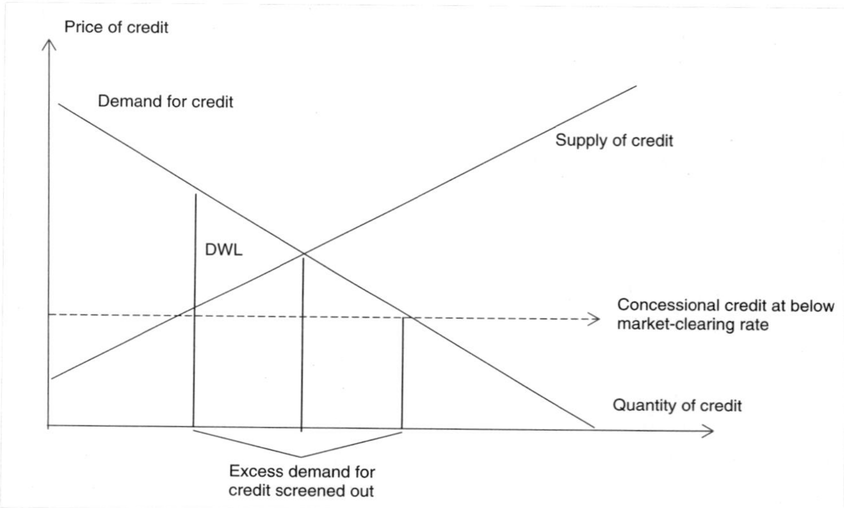

Fig. 9.1: Partial Equilibrium Approach to Credit, Resulting in Deadweight Loss (DWS) from Confessional Credit

The second myth of formal creditor tends to get belied as soon as he confronts resource-poor borrowers, who have neither a marketable collateral, nor a credit-worthy project to satisfy him for issuing a loan. It is therefore no surprise that in order to pressurize formal banking sector to provide loans to resource-poor borrowers, government has to declare concessional rates and impose statutory obligations for making priority sector lending and even to announce occasional loan waiver/relief schemes to relieve poor borrowers of their accumulated debts. While the commercial banking sector including RRBs are major victims of these two above-stated myths, the cooperative banking sector also is not totally free from the same maladies, even though cooperative lenders have definitely some local comparative advantages as compared to the commercial banking sector. Interestingly, the non-formal sector—whether government/NABARD/NGO-promoted MFIs or NBFC-promoted MFIs or even a large array of informal moneylenders, on the other hand, are continuously busy, using their local and intimate knowledge about borrowers, in evolving systems and processes to tackle the above-stated loopholes of a credit contract. As a result, even though our policy makers are always keen to wish them away, these non-formal sources have not only created a niche for themselves, but also are resilient to most changes in credit policy. This has happened more frequently in a rural context, where market imperfections and market failures, better understood by these non-formal sectors, are order of the day. In other words, the prolonged existence and even growth of non-formal sources is a response to a colossal failure of the formal credit sector to understand and appreciate certain basics in credit. This is the basic conclusion; the present study arrives at, after a careful review of the findings of this study.

Once the above-stated myths are removed, it is not difficult to understand the following four propositions, which arise out of this study:

1. The different credit sources are not always in competitive relation with each other;
2. No single source has point wise superiority over others;
3. These sources arise and function steadily without much of government subsidies, just because they enjoy certain comparative advantages in local scenarios, and often act in response to certain glaring and persistent shortfalls of formal sector credit; and
4. Given rationing of loan by formal sources, these sources often come to the rescue of rural borrowers, thus implying that these sources stand in complementary relationship with each other from the viewpoint of a resource-poor or even a typical rural borrower.

Before we spell out the recommendations arising out of this study in greater detail, it is important to reiterate the major conclusions arising out of chapters 3 to 8, to refresh reader's mind and to facilitate his understanding of the recommendations which follow:

1. On access to credit, relatively cheap commercial banks cum RRB source, generally raises strong expectations in the minds of rural borrowers as highly potential source of credit, but these expectations are often belied for most of the rural clients, except for some affluent sections among these borrowers. The other five sources, and especially formal-2 and informal-2 provide easy access. Between the two i.e., between informal-2 and formal-2, the former provides a much easier access, while the latter has a bias in favor of landed classes of borrowers. Well-functioning cooperatives as well as newly evolved semiformal sectors (i.e., MFIs promoted by Government/ NABARD/NGO or NBFCs) seem to have restricted the penetration

of the informal source to some extent and found to be providing good competition, especially to the traditional informal lenders.

2. Since credit is a package of services with multifarious attributes, the non-formal sources and especially the two informal sources, due to their proximity to and intimacy with local borrowers, are in a much stronger position compared to others to have minute variations in these terms and conditions to suit the preferences of rural borrowers and charge a suitable price accordingly. At times, the non-formal sources charge exorbitant rates with stringent conditions, but they too have the flexibility of charging a zero rate of interest in certain occasions. The two semi-formal sources, even though their credit schemes are uniform for all borrowing, are also in a position to impart some flexibility especially in repayment schedule under contingent situation. This, they are there to compete with the two informal sources, and especially with informal-1, while filling in the deficiencies of the two formal sources to provide credit to those, who cannot access formal sources for one reason or the other. Interestingly, there seems to be a natural division of labor across these various sources—while the commercial banking sector has specialized in supply of large loans for production and human capital investment purposes with low percentage transaction cost, the cooperative sector provides small to medium size loans, again, mainly for production purposes (though often deliberately allowing a small component of consumption loan through adverse use of production loan). The two informal sources as well as two semi-formal sources seem to have specialized in supplying mainly small, but sometimes up to medium size loans, for all purposes.
3. In terms of observable and measurable attributes of borrower transaction cost, it is seen that these costs are much higher on per loan basis, but considerably lower as proportion of loan amount, for formal sources as compared to semi-formal and informal sources. This is precisely why large and medium borrowers with suitable collaterals and projects are found to gather around formal lenders, while most small and medium borrowers without marketable collateral gather around semi-formal and informal sources. It is therefore natural to argue in favor of placing this observed pattern on a sound and healthier basis based on policy support.
4. Given the observed difficulties of borrowers in making use of their production loan, which they are often required to handle on their own, it is not surprising that they would be looking for supplies of credit complementary services from their usually resource-rich

lenders. Multipurpose PACS are found to be doing this job pretty well, charging even lower prices for the complementary inputs. Sometimes, informal lenders, too, are found to be doing the same thing, but not necessarily at below market price. Some semi-formal-2 sources like BASIX and Bandhan are found to be supplying credit plus services, through making parallel arrangements with a third party. Semi-formal-1 source is yet to de the same on a significant scale.

5. Regarding supply of extension services in the context of rural credit, one is shocked to see that borrower's utilization of, incurred expenditure on, and familiarity with official sources of extension services related to agriculture, allied activities including fisheries, group formation and some general services, are pretty low. While good cooperatives are found to be providing some extension services, they are often constrained to scale up this service, while yet to use records of borrower's response to extension for purpose of monitoring loans in a formal way. The two semi-formal sources seem to be using extension mostly for the purpose of monitoring, rather than using it as a positive input to augment borrower's productivity in the existing line of production or to induce them towards higher lines of production. In case of informal sectors, extension service is absolutely on an informal basis. Obviously, there is ample scope for improving extension service both in terms of quality and dimensions of coverage, and putting it on a strong institutional basis linked with credit.
6. Quite shockingly, the study has found that the loan waiver/relief scheme is a major misnomer, which may confer political gains to the parties in power, but with hardly any benefit or change in the fortunes of poor borrowers. Although, the meager benefits have largely flown to small farmers, but their transaction cost in realizing this benefit also seems pretty large.

9.7 RECOMMENDATIONS

While spelling out the recommendations arising out of this study, the main issue is whether to destroy knowingly or unknowingly the observed complementarity across various credit sources, which arise out of specific comparative advantages of each sector, or to promote a careful and healthy growth of all these sectors together. The authors' recommendations based on different segments' comparative strengths and weaknesses are summarized in Table 9.1.

Table 9.1: Policy Recommendations for Different Segments of Rural Credit

Rural Credit Segments	*Major Strengths*	*Major Weaknesses*	*Recommendations*
1. Formal-1: Commercial banks and RRBs	(i) Collateral and/or sound project based large loans at concessional rates and at low percentage transaction cost to itself and to its borrowers; (ii) higher-tiers can easily perform functions of development banking as well as of regulatory authorities to ensure accountability of lower-tiers as well as large individual and organizational borrowers.	(i) Observed bias in favor of large and affluent individuals as well as organizational borrowers; (ii) follows 'minimalist credit' rather than 'credit-plus' approach.	1. Government must permanently discard loan waiver/relief schemes, leaving such compassionate acts to discretion of banks (govt. can at most request) to follow in cases of extreme emergency in identified pockets; 2. Concentrate on sound project based and collateral based loans without being influenced by political rhetoric and ideological overtones—thus following purely age old banking principles; 3. Must produce research-based sector studies, strategy materials, regulatory systems and processes, and useful extension materials, using a stakeholder approach; 4. Should start lending to semi-formal-2 and two informal sources as well, to encourage accountability, transparency and competition, while straightening out the modalities of credit/refinance to formal-2 and semi-formal-1 segments.
2. Formal-2: Cooperative banks	(i) Good at providing small to medium size loans with a small consumption component, at low transaction cost and as credit plus provider.	(i) General bias against landless, allied and non-farm borrowers; (ii) almost always suffers from generic sectorial deficiencies with respect to geographic coverage, accessing capital, employee incentives, brand building, autonomy, etc.	1. Constitutional protection needed to bring autonomy back replacing current para-statal status in most cases. 2. Innovative reforms needed torelax/remove geographic limitations, encourage capital flow within cooperatives, access capital from market, promote brand development, provide performance-linked incentives and promotional opportunities to retain/attract beautiful professional minds as employees—thus to provide a level playing field vis-à-vis the corporate sector. 3. Reform measure may necessitate movement from old fashioned puritan form of cooperative to a more composite

Table contd...

Table 9.1 contd...

Rural Credit Segments	*Major Strengths*	*Major Weaknesses*	*Recommendations*
			kind of structure combining the strong points of both coops and corporates, as seen in Japanese form of organizations called *keiretsu*, and more commonly referred to as stakeholder cooperatives. 4. Must promote SHGs by building bridges with semi-formal-1 not only to rope in landless as well as multifarious allied and non-farm borrowers, but also to provide healthy competition to the fast-growing semi-formal-2 segment. 5. Must switch back to leader-driven from current state-driven mode, as used to be the case during 1950s and 1960s, before massive government intervention and support started subverting their autonomous status.
3. Semi-formal-1: Govt./NABARD/ NGO-promoted MFIs	(i) Can use thrift and peer pressure based monitoring processes to make small loans for consumption and petty production purposes at low transaction cost and negligible default rate; (ii) good for leadership development at grass-root level, especially among women.	(i) Bank-SHG linkage sometimes goes against the source, thus relegating it to the status of net creditors to banks; (ii) needs persistently strong promotional inputs from local level NGOs; (iii) generally lacks knowledge based extension inputs for spiral growth.	1. Needs handholding of well-known NGOs and coops like SEWA, Pradhan, BASIX Livelihood School, Mulukanoor, Warana, Amalsad, etc. and support of premium educational institutes across the country to gradually develop these organizations and their higher tier bodies. 2. Must aspire to have their own banks at the earliest possible opportunity as SEWA and Warana did. 3. Must gradually but steadily move toward larger size production loans to promote value added products and capture premium niche markets. 4. Must promote their higher tier bodies, not only to suit economics of value added products (as in case of AMUL), but also to undertake lobbying activities to safeguard their interest.
4. Semi-formal-2: NBFC-promoted MFIs	(i) Uses strong monitoring as well as group peer pressure to make both consumption and production loans at low	(i) Alleged to be using coercive methods of loan repayment, and charges exorbitant	1. Government and policy makers must change their mindset towards this fast growing segment by (a) recognizing NBFC-MFIS as an important instrument for achieving financial inclusiveness, (b) appreciating their capacity in generating

Table contd...

Table 9.1 contd…

Rural Credit Segments	*Major Strengths*	*Major Weaknesses*	*Recommendations*
	transaction cost as well as low default rate; (ii) some of them have started providing credit-plus services to rope in even hardcore poor with the aim of lifting them into the mainframe economy; (iii) some have developed capacity, interest as well as urge to make larger size production loans to support a spiral process of growth of customers.	interest and other charges, which are not always sufficiently transparent; (ii) extension is more monitoring- oriented rather than oriented towards production of knowledge based value added items for premium market segments.	multiplier effect for growth and development of local economies through infusion of hard outside money to promote credit-starved various non-standard projects, and (c) evolving, through open dialogues and consultations, a friendly rather than a repressive system of regulations, which would appreciate their roles, and give them the necessary space, instead of over-reacting to certain isolated aberrations, as reported in this segment. 2. These MFIs themselves must move towards a more transparent and accountable system by evolving self-regulatory mechanisms through creation of suitable higher-tier bodies and taking help of well-known national and international bodies, NGOs, coops (e.g. RABO Bank), and even corporates working in this field. 3. These MFIs must train their field staff in knowledge based extension to enable their clients to move towards production of value added and branded items to gradually penetrate premium markets or market segments. 4. Both semi-formal-1 and semi-formal-2 segments, as they grow, must strive towards developing People's Universities and Management Institutes to strengthen their own R&D, on the one hand, and to enable free inflow and outflow of knowledge or information to gain more acceptability to the public and thus to sustain their growth, on the other. 5. Must develop their federations, besides linkages with premium educational institutions and business associations, to safeguard their interests. 6. This segment too may be allowed to take deposits from clients even on a limited scale, as provided in the Draft Microfinance Bill of 2010, to generate competition to the

Table contd…

Table 9.1 contd…

Rural Credit Segments	*Major Strengths*	*Major Weaknesses*	*Recommendations*
			formal segments, which can have 'financial inclusiveness' only in terms of deposit collection, but not in terms of loan disbursal. 7. A certain % of public sector commercial banks may be dispensed through MFIS, besides making NABARD refinance for non-farm activities of poor households available to them.
5. Informal-1: **Traditional Rural Moneylenders**	(i) Provides small to medium size loans for all purposes together with necessary credit-plus services at flexible terms and conditions and at low transaction cost; (ii) resilient to changes in policy environment.	(i) Hard to locate in today's political and policy context; (ii) doesn't have scalability; (iii) age-old allegations of coercion, high interest rate and lack of transparency and accountability have created mindset unfavorable to their open existence and growth.	1. (also 6.1) Government and policy makers must give up their traditional hostility and intolerant attitude towards these two segments and must be prepared to (i) rope them in through liberal credit linkage with the commercial banking sector, (ii) evolve suitable regulatory systems through close interactions, and (iii) promote accountability, transparency and competitiveness in their operations.
6. Informal-2: **Other Local Lenders—Friends, Relatives, Input Dealers, Grocery Shopkeepers, Medical Stores, Cloth Merchants etc.**	(i) Provides flexible small to large size loans usually in kind and mostly for consumption purposes at extremely low transaction cost; (ii) have sometimes capability to provide not only monitoring-oriented, but also productivity/value-augmenting extension; (iii) highly resilient to changes in policy environment.	(i) Usually the same criticisms, as levied against informal-1 segment, are applied, without being able to clearly distinguish between this segment from informal-1 segment.	

References

Bardhan, P.K. (1989). A Note on Interlinked Rural Economic Arrangements. In P. Bardhan (ed.) The Economic Theory of Agrarian Institutions (pp. 237–242). Oxford: Clarendon Press.

Bardhan, P.K. and Rudra, A. (1978). Interlinkage of Land, Labour and Credit Relations: An Analysis of Village Survey Data in East India. *Economic and Political Weekly,* 13(6/7), 367–384.

Basu, K. (1983). The Emergence of Isolation and Interlinkage in Rural Market. *Oxford Economic Papers*, 35(2), 262–80.

Basu, P. (2005). A Financial System for India's Poor. Economic and Political Weekly, September 10, 4008–4012.

Basu, S. (1997). Why Institutional Credit Agencies are Reluctant to Lend to the Rural Poor: A Theoretical Analysis of the Indian Rural Credit Market. World Development, 25(2), 267–280.

Bell, C. (1990). Interactions between Institutional and Informal Credit Agencies in Rural India. *World Bank Economic Review*, 4 (3), 297–327.

Besley, T. and Coate, S. (1995). Group Lending, Repayment Incentives and Social Collateral. *Journal of Development Economics*, 46, 1–18.

Bhaumik, S.K. and Rahim, A. (1999). Interlinked Credit Transactions in Rural West Bengal. *Indian Journal of Agricultural Economics*, 54(2), 169–184.

Braverman, A. and Gausch, J.L. (1984). Capital Requirements, Screening and Interlinked Sharecropping and Credit Contracts. *Journal of Development Economics,* 14(3), 359–74.

Dasgupta, *et al.* (1989). Report on Informal Credit Markets in India: Summary, National Institute of Public Finance and Policy, New Delhi.

Datta, S.K. (1992). Understanding Rural Money lenders—A Study of Two Villages from West Bengal. Study sponsored by NABARD. Ahmedabad: Indian Institute of Management.

Datta, S.K. (2003). An Institutional Economics Approach to the Problems of Small Farmer Credit in India. Working Paper 2003-07-01, Ahmedabad: Indian Institute of Management.

Dev, S.M. (2008). Agriculture: Absence of a Big Push. *Economic and Political Weekly,* 43(15), 33–39.

EPW Research Foundation (2008). The Loan Waiver Scheme. Economic and Political Weekly, 43(11), 28–34.

Fisher, T. and Sriram, M.S. (2002). Beyond Micro-Credit: Putting Development Back into Micro-Finance. New Delhi: Sage Publications (Vistaar Imprint).

Ghate, P.B. (1988). Informal Credit Markets in Asian Developing Countries. Asian Development Review, Vol. 6, No. 1, pp. 64–85.

Gill, A. (2004). Interlinked Agrarian Credit Markets: Case Study of Punjab. Economic and Political Weekly, 39(33), 3741–3751.

Iqbal, F. (1988). The Determinants of Moneylender Interest Rates: Evidence from Rural India. *Journal of Development Studies,* 24(3), 364–78.

Mahajan, V. and Ramola, B.G. (2003). Financial Services For The Rural Poor and Women in India: Access And Sustainability. Background paper prepared for the World Bank. Washington D.C.: World Bank.

Morduch, J. (1999). The Microfinance Promise. Journal of Economic Literature, 37 (December), 1569–1614.

Qureshi, S., Nabi, I. and Faruqee, R.R. (1996). Rural Finance for Growth and Poverty Alleviation. World Bank Policy Research Working Paper No. 1593 (April).

Rath, N. (2009). Implications of the Loan Waiver for Rural Credit Institutions. Economic and Political Weekly, 43 (24), 13–16.

Ray, D. (1998). Development Economics. New Delhi: Oxford University Press.

Reddy, S.T.S. (2007). Diary of a Moneylender. Economic and Political Weekly, July 21, 3037–3043.

Reddy, Y.V. (2001). Indian Agriculture and Reform: Concern, Issues and Agenda, RBI Bulletin, March.

Sarap, K. (1990). Factors Affecting Small Farmers' Access to Institutional Credit in Rural Orissa, India. Development and Change, 21(2), 281–307.

Sarap, K. (1991). Interlinked Agrarian Markets in Rural India. New Delhi: Sage Publications.

Swaminathan, M. (1991). Segmentation, Collateral Undervaluation and the Rate of Interest in Agrarian Credit Markets: Some Evidence from Two Villages in South India. *Cambridge Journal of Economics,* 15(2), 161–178.

Timberg, T.A. and Aiyar, C.V. (1984). Informal Credit Markets in India. Economic Development and Cultural Change, Vol. 33, No. 1, pp. 43–59.